Miss Lyla's Papers

A Posthumous History of **Iuka, Mississippi**

–

Tales with Native American Roots, Civil War Battles,
and Healing Mineral Waters Arise with a Clear Voice
from a Box of Crumbling Papers

Compiled

by

Billie Burke, Eddie and Frank Thomas

Pearl Street Publishing

Miss Lyla's Papers

Author: Lyla Merrill McDonald

Compiled and edited:
Billie Burke, Eddie and Frank Thomas

Typesetting and Cover design: Frank Thomas

Cover Photograph: Billie Burke Thomas

First Edition

Publication Date: Feb. 14 – *Valentine's Day* – 2024

Library of Congress Control Number: 2024901095

ISBN-13: 978-1-885154-71-2 (softcover)

Printed in the United States of America

Pearl Street Publishing
P. O. Box 153
Iuka, MS 38852
USA

To
Appreciate and Remember

Mrs. Lyla McDonald

On November 25, 1949, Miss Lyla spoke at the dedication of
the Mississippi Historical Marker placed at the gate of the
Iuka Mineral Springs Park. Billie Burke Thomas was in the
audience and snapped this front cover photograph.

May you never forget what is
worth remembering, nor ever
remember what is best forgotten.

- an Irish Blessing

Prologue

Whoever brought the large, dilapidated cardboard box full of old, brown paper in the backdoor of our house was ready to set it down. They scooted it the last foot or so over by the window. I don't remember when this was; probably the early to middle 1980s, give or take.

Mother was in the kitchen and pointed. "The bottom is about to fall out of that."

"What is it?" I asked.

"Miss Lyla's papers."

"Who?"

"Lyla McDonald. You remember Miss Lyla. The McDonald home?"

I vaguely remembered her. The McDonald home I remembered better. It was a sprawling antebellum home next to the Iuka High School with a circle of columns around its porch.

I was in school in Iuka, Mississippi, from 1952 through 1964 and remember the McDonald home as quiet and distant compared to the hustle and bustle of a first through twelfth-grade schoolyard. An unwritten rule said the

McDonald's yard was off-limits. Everybody respected it. Even when walking to town after school, everybody went down the sidewalk. Nobody cut across their yard. Occasionally, Miss Lyla puttered around outside, but not often. I don't remember Mr. McDonald.

Lyla McDonald was born Lyla Merrill in Iuka in 1876. The Merrill home was across the street from the McDonald home and about a hundred yards to the west. Small world. Miss Lyla graduated from the Iuka Normal Institute and married Tom McDonald in 1899. The McDonalds bought the Lyle home, which before that was the Moore home because Colonel John Lawrence Moore built it in 1858-59. For the rest of its existence, the Lyle/Moore home was the McDonald home.

Miss Lyla published a book in the 1920s called *Iuka's History*.

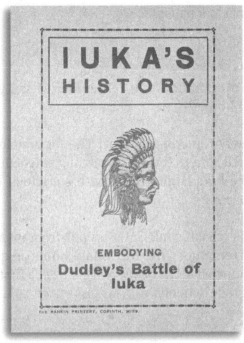

She wrote articles for regional newspapers and speeches which she gave. Her subject was almost always the same—local history. With pencil and pen, she scribbled notes in interviews, copied facts from books and newspapers and jotted down what she heard and thought. Sometimes she organized it; sometimes, she didn't. It seems she absorbed local history all her life.

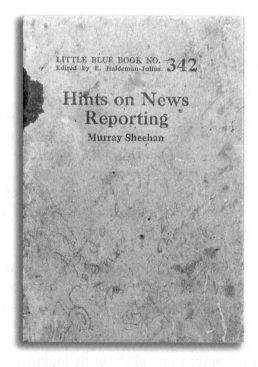

A copy of a TEN CENT POCKET SERIES LITTLE BLUE BOOK NO. 342 Copyright 1922 – *Hints on News Reporting* by Murray Sheehan found in Miss Lyla's papers. Sample chapters are "What is News?" "What Interests People?" "Accuracy First."

Tom McDonald died in 1960; Miss Lyla in 1962. In the 1980s, this old cardboard box filled with newspaper clippings, brochures, photographs, pamphlets, and page after page of Miss Lyla's handwritten and typed notes, ended up inside our backdoor.

I was still looking down at the box. "Where'd this come from?"

"Miss Lyla gave it to Aline Jackson, across the street from her house. She hoped Aline would do something with it, but Jim (Aline's son) said Aline wasn't going to do anything and gave it to me."

"What are you going to do?"

"Don't know. Read some of it."

I lost track, but over the next few years, Mother, Billie Burke Thomas, read it all. She first placed each page of what, in some cases, is century-old, crumbling paper into plastic notebook sleeves and then in manila folders. On the folders, she wrote comments. Several years ago, while cleaning out our mother's home after her death, my brother, Frank, and I discovered all these folders, neatly stacked, a couple of feet high.

We placed them into another cardboard box. In time we read it all, and in more time, we typed it into a computer. Along the way, and quite by accident, we discovered that even though most of the pages started and stopped in mid-sentence and, for the most part, seemed random with lots missing, some of them fit together, making longer documents, some as many as thirty pages—quite a puzzle. Luck and clues like degrees of aging paper, similarities in pencil scribbles, and the color of pen ink helped solve some mysteries. Eventually, stories rose from hundreds of seemingly unrelated pages. From a scattered garden came flowers.

Iuka, Mississippi, has only one history. Miss Lyla told it over and over again for different reasons and at different lengths. She rarely placed dates on anything, and like all Southern ladies, she was good at disguising age. Besides the dozens of booklets, pamphlets and newspaper clippings written by others, there was a lifetime, hundreds of pages, of Miss Lyla's words in that cardboard box. Frank and I tried to piece together one chronological history from her mountain of work, telling each of her stories and anecdotes only once. That was nearly impossible. She could wind a good tale, so good it was hard to snake pieces out.

In **Miss Lyla's Papers,** you will find some tales told more than once, but they are Miss Lyla's tales, saying, "This is the way it was back then." Sometimes her stories overlap, or they repeat. And yet even with the duplications, there are times they light up like fireworks. Also, the **APPENDIX** is more than just additional information. It contains details – a mountain of interesting, in-depth, decades-old details.

From a box of unorganized work, our mother read, took notes and organized. From her stack of manila folders and plastic sleeves and with the assistance of technology and the methods of Sherlock Holmes, Frank and I are glad to again let Miss Lyla speak, mostly in her own words, and tell us "how it was back then."

All that is well and good, but I believe I would be misrepresenting what is presented in this book if I didn't say, after years of work and research and getting to know Miss Lyla quite well through her words, I find she may be overly fond of her community at times, so much so that often when she had the chance to make it look better, she did. She was a cheerleader. She quoted few sources, was prone to exaggerate, and could easily stretch a good tale. At times she was careless, and other times, I can't be sure, but disregarding these papers due to any shortcomings would be shortsighted, so we chose to overlook their overstatements and share them. Most of this is a spot-on history of Iuka, Mississippi, and the surrounding area. Read thoughtfully, be mindful of what you are reading and be patient. Miss Lyla was the queen of writing in passive voice, and her enthusiasm for painting vast landscapes in these working notes could make her sentences run on to be paragraphs.

Miss Lyla left no bibliography or footnotes, only a box of fragile paper that, after a century, has turned golden brown, or maybe I should simply say, golden. Picture her in the dim light of the McDonald home, writing from her heart and memory with pencil, pen and typewriter. That is **Miss Lyla's Papers**.

Eddie Thomas

Contents

CHAPTER 1

MRS. LYLA MCDONALD

Miss Lyla circa 1957 on the porch of the McDonald Home

"Should you ask me whence this story, whence the legends and traditions I would answer from the hillsides, from the red hills of Mississippi, from the lakes which surround it, from the hills of Tishomingo where the Red Man once had wandered."

Lyla McDonald

CHAPTER 2

GENIE FROM A CARDBOARD BOX

(Touch a few brittle, musty pages. Take a deep breath...)

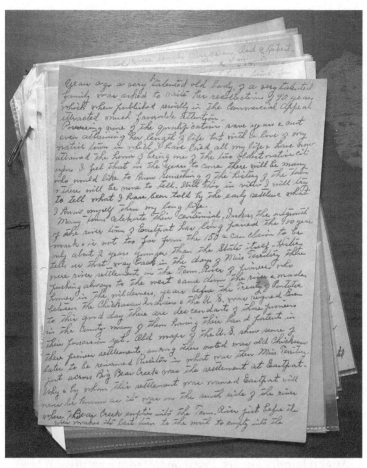

(If touch and smell could be captured and passed along, they would be placed here at the beginning, but hopefully, a glance at Miss Lyla's handwriting and typing will be enough to stir your senses.)

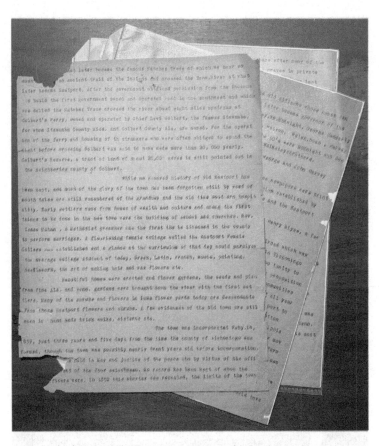

(Miss Lyla wrote a history of Iuka in 1924.
After a hundred years, like a genie from a cardboard box,
she writes another.)

CHAPTER 3

CHICKASAW INDIANS OF THE
MISSISSIPPI-ALABAMA TERRITORY

*(The first article transcribed for Miss Lyla's Papers is one
she entitled CHICKASAW INDIANS OF THE MISS – ALA
TERRITORY. These three faded, tattered, typed pages were
once held together with a rusty paperclip and appear from
their condition to be among her earliest writings.)*

I have selected for my story a most intriguing yet most
baffling subject; the Chickasaw chiefs whose names we
call daily but about whom there is a cloak of such heavy
folds that no one lifts the covers. Although these chiefs
have been dead less than a century, and our ancestors
must have known them personally, little or no word is
left to tell of their prowess. Whether our ancestors were
too busy carving homes out of the wilderness that they
had taken from the Indians or whether they thought all
Indians were bad Indians and should quickly be forgotten,
we know not, but we do know all too well that there is a
paucity of information about those with whom we should
be most familiar and whose names we keep alive in the
towns and counties of our own and adjoining states.

The first I shall notice is Tashka Ambi, The Warrior
Who Kills. The village of Tuscumbia, Alabama, was first
known as Oka Kapassa and was destroyed by General

Robertson of Tennessee in 1787. Later a white settler named Dickson, who passed the Big Spring on his way to New Orleans with General Andrew Jackson, came there to live. Other white settlers followed, and a contest was on for naming the new town. The choice lay between Anniestown for the little daughter of Dickson and the Indian. The Indian name was chosen by one vote, and so pleased was the chief that he gave the little girl beads and furs. Tashka Ambi has been corrupted into Tuscumbia.

Colbert County, in the extreme northwest corner of Alabama, shares a border with Tishomingo County, Mississippi, and is named for a famous Chickasaw Indian family. Logan James Colbert, a Scotch adventurer driven by wanderlust, left the Carolinas and came to the Indian village in Muscle Shoals. He was adopted by the Indians and made a chief. Later he married three Indian maids. Two of them were full-blooded Chickasaw, and the third was a half-breed. He was the father of eight children, amassed a fortune and owned many slaves. Logan Colbert once led an expedition against the Americans at Fort Jefferson and received a bullet wound in his hand.

In 1784, while on his way from the Chickasaw Nation to Georgia, Logan Colbert was killed, supposedly by his slave, Caesar, who reported that his master fell from his horse.

George Colbert, the son of Logan Colbert, was born in what is now Lauderdale County, Alabama. He became a man of great influence and wealth by running a ferry at Colbert Shoals where the Natchez Trace crosses the Tennessee River. Legend has it that he was paid $20,000 annually in ferry fees. An interesting feature about the old home of George Colbert is the fact that it was built at Ross' Landing where Chattanooga now stands, loaded on a flat boat and rafted down the Tennessee River to Colbert Ferry where it still stands after about 136 years. The Alabama D.A.R. has marked the spot.

Personal reminiscences of an old citizen of Florence, Alabama, describe George Colbert as tall, slender, handsome and somewhat lighter in color than the full-blooded Chickasaws. He wore the dress of a white man and was always neat and clean. He went west with his tribe and died in the new nation in 1839.

A more famous Colbert was Levi Colbert, who lived at Buzzard Roost Creek near Barton, Alabama. A marker has also been erected there. Levi Colbert later moved to Mississippi, where he became known as Itawamba. The county to the south of us bears his name. Itawamba means Sitting Chief or Bench Chief and was a special designation for some signal service he had rendered. Itawamba, with his brothers, was in the War of 1812 with General Andrew Jackson and never tired of talking of the old wars as he called them.

He had three wives, two were sisters, and all lived in the greatest affection. The children were taught obedience to all the women, the same as to their own mother.

Levi Colbert was a wealthy man, owning over 20,000 acres of land in Alabama alone, 4,000 head of cattle and 120 slaves. Both whites and Indians respected him. Several of his children married into some of the best families in the state. One of his daughters, Vici, was in love with Colonel James Gordon, owner of Lochinvar and is the heroine of a lovely poem written by Mrs. Dabney Anderson of Pontotoc. Itawamba died at the home of one of his married daughters near Tuscumbia, Alabama, while on his way to Washington to see about some Indian affairs.

7

When Tecumseh, the famous Shawnee chief and orator, visited the Chickasaw Nation to enlist the tribe against the American colonists, it was the Colberts, Piomingo and our own Tishomingo who would not let him talk, saying that their tribe had always been friendly toward the Americans, that they had fought in the same wars, were as brothers and hoped to stay that way.

Of our own chiefs, Iuka and Tishomingo, I have learned little. No history I have found mentions Iuka, so he must have been one of the lesser lights in the nation. All that we know is the legend we were told as children viz: Iuka, sick and suffering with a baffling malady and nearly blind, was brought on the litter to the springs near the Tennessee River. After drinking the health-giving waters and bathing his weak eyes in the spring, which ever after bore the name of the Eye Spring, he was cured. He became so enamored with the beautiful spot that here he built his home. In the streams, which abounded with all kinds of fish, and the beautiful forests, he found all that made life desirable. Here he lived and died, and here he is buried. To the town's early inhabitants, his burial ground was pointed out as being under what is now the post office. To children, this was a spot of awe. A favorite story told was that if you went to the grave and asked Iuka what killed him he would answer Nothing. Several years ago, when the building was demolished, no trace of a grave was found.

Early settlers of the town in plowing their gardens often excavated graves, so the spot must have been the scene of many a sanguinary conflict. Further evidence of this is found in the large number of arrowheads uncovered. The three mountain peaks west of town also show evidence of conflicts, and there is no doubt that many a bloody battle took place in this area.

Iuka and Tishomingo were great friends, and to these healing waters Tishomingo often came to be with his friend and to be benefited from the mineral waters which even then were of recognized worth.

A story told by the early settlers which shows the beautiful spirit of hospitality among the Indians and also shows the friendship between the two chiefs is that a white man coming from Cotton Gin Port on the Tombigbee River fell among thieves who robbed him of all he possessed and like the thieves of Jericho left the man to die on the road. He was found by Tombigbee, the son-in-law of Tishomingo, and nursed back to health. Tombigbee then took him to the home of Tishomingo where he was given a personal escort to the home of Iuka. Iuka rendered more aid before providing protection to the home of Tashka Ambi. Had an Indian fallen among thieves would white men have been as willing to render aid and protection to him?

CHAPTER 4

JACINTO

(These three typed pages have several pencil and pen corrections as though they were Miss Lyla's handheld notes for a speech.)

OLD TISHOMINGO

I am grateful for the privilege of addressing descendants of the Old Free State of Tishomingo. This area of almost a million acres was part of the vast region acquired by the Treaty of Pontotoc from the Chickasaw Indians in 1832. It was appropriately named for a worthy old warrior chief of those Indians.

Soon after the county was organized in 1836, the county fathers selected a central site for a seat of government. Armstead Barton donated 60 acres of land for the projected town, which leaders hastily named Cincinnati. Then it occurred to some that it would be inappropriate for the United States to have two great cities bearing the same name. About this time, Sam Houston won a victory over Santa Anna at San Jacinto, giving your ancestors the opportunity to honor their promising little city with a glorious name.

From Armstead Barton's generous gift, 53 lots were sold for some $10,000. $199.00 of this money was used to build a log courthouse. Almost as much was required to "rail" the building in 1841.

Other public edifices were promptly erected. In November 1836, John Fitch paid $74.00 a year to operate the first tavern. A few months later, a jail was constructed for just under $4,000. Then Samuel Carson opened an inn toward the close of 1837. But more important for the citizens were the saw and gristmills that had operated from the beginning.

Life in Old Tishomingo, judged by our standards, was hard. There were no carbonated drinks, ice, anesthesia, fancy foods, elite recreation or easy transportation. Even many of our necessities were unknown to them. Although they followed the time-honored custom of "jugging" their corn, it was not until January 1842 that the first saloon was licensed, shortly before six ministers were authorized to perform marriage ceremonies. But business was so good that two other saloons were opened the following April. It was sometime before the first church building was erected. The Methodists allowed all denominations to use their edifice, but the Baptists built one of their own in 1845.

Overseers had been looking after the needy since January 1838. In 1846, a Poor House was constructed for $50.00.

But most of the people were prospering, and Jacinto was growing. While the majority lived in log dwellings, leaders came to believe that justice should be meted out in a more dignified structure. Consequently, the "palatial" brick courthouse was opened just a hundred years ago. It cost exactly $6,798 and was paid for when completed.

This building was designed for serious business with no shows or like entertainment being permitted.

2

Going shopping apparently never occurred to your grandmothers, or their mothers of the 1830s, 1840s and 1850s. Why should they have thought of such a thing when G. W. Norton, the peddler, was allowed to use a four-wheeled wagon to carry goods to their doors?

Two newspapers, the Democrat and the Reporter, appeared in Jacinto in 1849, but it was several months before news began to drift over a telegraph line to the office in Jacinto. Now guests in the Jacinto Hotel could report their arrival to well-wishers a thousand miles away.

In 1846, with three saloons, two taverns, two churches and an escape-proof jail in operation, the county fathers provided for school commissioners. A decade later, John F. Arnold and others opened the Jacinto Male Academy, which soon became a renowned institution. Two years later, no one could teach in Old Tishomingo without a license.

The people were justifiably proud of their achievements but eager to do more. Hence they held their first county fair in 1858. Not to be left behind, the doctors formed a county medical association two years later.

Your father's grandfathers cleared the wilderness, built roads and bridges and erected brick public buildings while most lived in log dwellings. Hunting the abundant bears, panthers, deer and turkey was a business for them rather than a pastime. Wolves were such a nuisance that the county paid for their scalps in 1840 and 1841. With the aid of slaves, those frontiersmen grew corn, peas, cotton, tobacco, wheat and vegetables. They shipped their surpluses from Eastport, whence also came some of their necessities. The women had to endure all the burdens of the frontier and also had to endure the pioneer men.

The railroads that entered the county in the middle of the 1850s brought Corinth, Iuka, Rienzi and other towns into being but doomed Eastport, Farmington, and Jacinto. The roads were also indirectly responsible for the division of the county in 1870.

The War for Southern Independence brought terrible times for Old Tishomingo. Several bloody battles were fought on its soil, including those of Corinth and Iuka. Hardly an able white man or boy was left at home. Townsfolk cared for the soldiers' families, although food was in short supply due to the war.

With the restoration of peace, people began a long struggle to recover from desolation. Food was soon in abundant supply. Good bacon could be bought in 1866 for 20¢ a pound, butter for 25¢, coffee for 33¢ and eggs for 20¢.

3

Building on foundations your ancestors left, you have established more attractive communities than they knew. Your ways of life are elegant beyond their powers to dream. Yet we should remember their dwelling places and honor them for their noble achievements.

CHAPTER 5

INCORPORATION OF EASTPORT

(A 1934 letter from Mississippi Secretary of State Walker Wood concerning the incorporation of Eastport, Mississippi)

Mississippi
Department of Secretary of State
Walker Wood, Secretary of State
Jackson, Mississippi

December 7, 1934

Mrs. T. M. McDonald
Iuka, Mississippi

Dear Mrs. McDonald:

Replying to your favor of December 4th: In re: Eastport, Tishomingo county:

So far as our records show, the Town of Eastport, Tishomingo County, was first incorporated by an Act of the Legislature of 1839, Chapter 134, approved February 14, 1839. This law provides for the town's incorporation and the election of the first officers, but does not name the officers. The law provided for an election to be held on the first Monday in May 1839, and that they should elect a justice of the peace, a constable and four selectmen, and that the Justice of the Peace, by virtue of his office, should be president of the board of selectmen.

This Act was repealed by an Act of the Legislature of 1852, and the town of Eastport was re-incorporated and the limits extended, and a governing body termed the Mayor and Board of Aldermen, but does not name the officers elected.

The municipal records of this office do not show any further reference to the Town of Eastport.

Complying with your request, I am today mailing you a copy of the Blue Book, and trust it will prove of value to you. Please accept it with my compliments.

Assuring you that it is always a pleasure to be of service to you, and with kind regards, I am

Yours very truly,

Walker Wood
Secretary of State

CHAPTER 6

EASTPORT – A RIVAL OF MEMPHIS

(These three, brittle, typed pages with bits of paper missing along the edges and corners are part of a larger document since page one begins in mid-sentence. Missing words or pieces of words were either obvious or taken from the information in the Walker Wood letter to Miss Lyla. Chapter 6 starts with the first complete paragraph on page one.)

While no recorded history of old Eastport has been kept, and much of the town's glory has been forgotten, still by word of mouth tales are remembered of the grandeur and the old-time Southern hospitality. Early settlers came from homes of wealth and culture, and among the first things done in the new town was the building of schools and churches. Reverend Isaac Mahan, a Methodist preacher, was the first to be licensed in the county to perform marriages. A flourishing female college called the Eastport Female College was established, and a glance at its curriculum would paralyze the average college students of today - Greek, Latin, French, music, painting, needlework, and the art of making hair and wax flowers.

Beautiful homes were erected, and flower gardens were grown. The seeds and plants from fine Alabama and Tennessee gardens came down the river with the first settlers. Many of the shrubs and flowers in Iuka today literally have their roots at Eastport. A few shreds of evidence, such as handmade brick walks and cisterns, remain in the old town.

Eastport was incorporated February 14, 1839, just three years and five days from the time the county of Tishomingo was formed, though the town was nearly twenty years old before incorporation. An election was held in May, and a justice of the peace became president of four selectmen. No record was kept of whom the first officers were. In 1852, this charter was repealed, the limits of the town extended and a mayor and aldermen elected.

Among the old citizens whose names can be recalled were Major J. M. Coman, John M. Stone, who later became governor of the state, Colonel Cal Terry, Colonel Winston Price, J. B. McKinney, William McKnight, George Hammerly, M. H. Wells, Sam DeWoody, Barnett, Castleberry, Brown, Nelson, Welch, Doan and Harvey.

Merchants who are remembered in the 1850s were McKnight and Son, Matthews and Doan, Price and Terry, Phillips and Son, and Walmsleys Brothers.

Two physicians are called to mind, Doctors George and John Harvey. The county has never had better medical men.

Three newspapers were printed in the town at various times. The Eastport North Mississippi Union established by M. G. Lewis in 1848, The Eastport Gazette in the early 50s and the Eastport Republican by W. H. H. Tison in 1851.

Henry Klyce operated a bookstore. A few books with his bookplate are still in existence.

With the proposed building of the Memphis and Charleston Railroad, the towns of Farmington and Eastport were offered, for a small concession of about $20,000, the opportunity to be placed on the map. Eastport's shortsighted citizens laughed the proposition to scorn, and Farmington did not see how it could be left off. Both communities paid with their lives for their lack of vision. Eastport was at the head of all-year navigation with an endless stream of wagons coming and going from the port to towns as far distant as Columbus, Mississippi. Thousands of bales of cotton came over the hills to be loaded for points as far away as Philadelphia and New York.

How could they foresee how soon rails would displace the slower moving boats? Soon the new towns of Burnsville, Corinth and Iuka replaced Farmington and Eastport. One became a settlement near Corinth; the other a memory of better days and one of the extinct towns of the state. Business houses and residences were torn down and brought to Iuka. Even the cemetery was desecrated by the plowshare after many of the dead were brought to Iuka and reinterred. A few scattering graves in private grounds are all that is left to show where first citizens slept their last sleep.

During the Civil War at least five battles or skirmishes were fought there. Bills to mark both the Eastport and Iuka battlefields were introduced in Congress years ago, but both died.

The Civil War finished the work of destruction that the building of the Memphis and Charleston Railroad began. Soon not a house was left in the town proper, and only a few outlying farmhouses remained.

And who among the dreamers but want can imagine how different life in this section might have been if the once prosperous town of Eastport, high on a bluff overlooking the Tennessee River, would have grown as did Memphis?

"The Rose Trail Drive by beautiful Pickwick Lake," from Wilmer Price's Illustrated Souvenir History of Iuka found in Miss Lyla's papers.

CHAPTER 7

RECOLLECTIONS OF EASTPORT

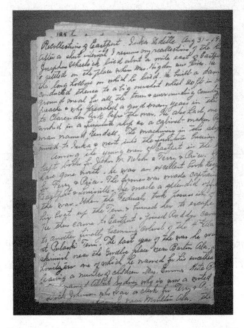

*(This article is one of several handwritten by Miss Lyla on one large piece of highly worn paper that initially could have been a blank sheet of newspaper. Three of these articles are Chapters 7, 9 and 21 of **Miss Lyla's Papers.***

These recollections of Eastport may have been written for the Vidette by Miss Lyla or copied from the Vidette. Either way, they appear to be recollections of R. L. McKnight and are enclosed here as written.)

20

Recollections of Eastport. Iuka Vidette. August 31, 1911. R L McKnight

After a short interval I resume my recollections of the historic town on the Tennessee River. Josephus Wheelock lived about a mile east of Eastport. He was one of the early settlers of the town and settled on the place where Mrs. Higdon now lives. He built a mill on the branch that runs down the long hollow on which he lived. He built a dam about 200 yards above the mill site and the water conducted thence to a big overshot wheel 20 feet in diameter that turned all the machinery. He ground meal for all the town and surrounding country. He had a son named John who was a Baptist preacher and who preached a good many years in this section. He also had two other sons who moved to Clarendon, Arkansas, before the war. He also had one daughter who married T. L. Collier. The latter worked in a furniture shop as a cabinetmaker. Collier worked in a shop in Eastport owned by a man named Kendall. The machinery in this shop was run by horse power. Collier afterwards moved to Iuka and went into the furniture business. He died in February 1905 leaving no descendants.

Among the young men of Eastport in the early days was John Smith an Irishman who kept books for John M. Nelson and Terry and Price. When the war came on he was supposed to have gone north. He was an excellent bookkeeper. W. A. Johnson and Dick Johnson were clerks for Terry and Price. The former was made captain of the steamer "Time" which ran between Eastport and Louisville. He made a splendid officer and ran on the boat until the beginning of the war. When the Federals took possession of the Ohio and Tennessee Rivers, Captain Johnson ran his boat up the Tennessee and burned her to escape capture by a gunboat which was in pursuit. He then came to Eastport and joined Roddey's cavalry and was afterwards promoted from one position to another finally becoming colonel of the 4th Alabama Cavalry. He was a brave officer and was wounded at Pulaski, Tennessee. The last year of the war he was married to Miss Kate Barton. During a skirmish near the Goodloe place near Barton, Alabama, he and his command captured two twelve pound howitzers one of which he named for his sweetheart. He died in Tuscumbia about 13 years ago leaving a number of children. Mrs. Emma Kate Bray of this place is a granddaughter. He had a son named Albert Sydney who is now a noted Presbyterian minister.

Dick Johnson, who was a clerk for Terry and Price, also joined Roddey's command. He was killed in a skirmish near Moulton, Alabama, the same skirmish in which W. E. McKinney was mortally wounded.

J. E. Johnson another brother was captain on the boat "W. T. Terry" and was in charge of the boat when it was captured at Paducah, Kentucky. He also became a member of Roddey's command and was captured at Bridgeport, Alabama, twelve miles east of Florence, Alabama, while the army was crossing the Tennessee River. He was carried to Rockford, Illinois, prison where he died of smallpox.

John Marshall Stone, afterwards colonel 2nd Mississippi and governor of the state, was a clerk for Terry and Price in those days. He came from Milan, Tennessee, when quite a young man and secured a position with this firm. In his conduct and management of the business entrusted to him he gave promise of the great ability that afterwards made him so famous in other fields of endeavor. In 1857 he came to Iuka. At the beginning of the war he raised a company in Iuka called the Iuka Rifles which afterwards became Company K 2nd Mississippi Infantry.

At the reorganization in Virginia he was elected colonel and served with conspicuous gallantry and distinction to the close of the war. His career in Mississippi politics is too well known to need setting forth in this article. He served his state faithfully and well and his body now rests in Oak Grove Cemetery.

Two other young men were clerks for Terry and Price in Eastport to wit: J. W. and George Latham who came from Waterloo, Alabama. They were both fine young men and highly thought of by all who knew them. Both these young men volunteered in Captain Stone's company and were killed in Virginia. Clay Terry a brother of J. C. Terry was also a member of the same company and fell victim to Federal bullets in Virginia.

CHAPTER 8

EASTPORT INHABITANTS

(Handwritten notes on the front and back of two small pages of lined paper appear to be from an interview. They are held together by a straight pen. Who Miss Lyla was interviewing isn't clear. Enclosed as written.)

The following facts given are very nearly all second hand information as I was only a boy of ten when Eastport was in its heyday. Am satisfied it is true.

The Business Men
John Briggs *Irishman* - merchant
James Burdwell was the first merchant

A. T. Matthews - merchant moved from Virginia to
       Athens, Alabama - marriage
H. L. Brown - merchant
Terry and Price - merchants and cotton buyers
Samuel DeWoody - postmaster and owner of local
       tavern
John M. Nelson - merchant cotton buyer
McMechan *Irishman* & Coman - merchants
James H. Doan - merchant
James Hill - livery man
Jesse Welch - saloon

Doctors
George and John Harvey *Irishmen*
A. M. Scruggs
---- Moore
Miller ----

Josephus Wheelock - owned an overshot mill fed by
water from a spring - sawed wood and ground wheat
and corn

***
Moses Curtis - wagoneer
Moses Terry - barber
Jim Anderson - shoemaker
Dorman Glover - finner
John Atkinson - drug Store
Henry Klein & Brothers - drug Store
Mr.--- Kendall - furniture - cabinetmaker

Methodist Church - Circuit
Garrett ----
David Mills

School - Public
Miss Tony DeWoody

Colonel Bill Johnson worked for Terry and Price, later
was captain of the Terry Steam boat that ran on the
Tennessee, Mississippi and Ohio Rivers. J. M. Stone
who later became a confederate colonel and then governor of Mississippi, worked on the Terry as clerk.

CHAPTER 9

RUINS OF EASTPORT

*(Miss Lyla's original cardboard box of papers revealed two
sources for the article Ruins of Eastport – one handwritten
on the same large piece of paper as the Recollections of
Eastport in Chapter 7 and the other in a crumbling issue of
the Vidette dated April 22, 1909.)*

Perched on an elevation in the fork of Bear Creek and
the Tennessee River and commanding a beautiful
view of the white capped-shoals in the distance where
the silver sheen of water is reflected on a clear day in
dazzling brilliancy, was the town of Eastport, once the
emporium of northeast Mississippi. A person familiar
with the place cannot but feel sad to wander over the site
of the once flourishing town and see the almost utter
desolation that now holds sway. Scarcely a vestige of the
old town remains. A few scattering cabins and an old,
dilapidated water mill remain in the suburbs, but of the
business part of town, which once contained 20 stores,
there is nothing left but a few brick bats. The plowshare
has torn up the ground where the main street once ran.
Preparations are being made to plant cotton where once
the busy tide of traffic and commerce ebbed and flowed.
A beautiful road runs from Iuka to Eastport. Along this
road in the fifties, an almost continuous stream of wagons
bumped along during the cotton season carrying the
fleecy staple and bringing back the necessities of life.

Now traveling that road you seldom meet more than two or three vehicles. – April 22, 1909

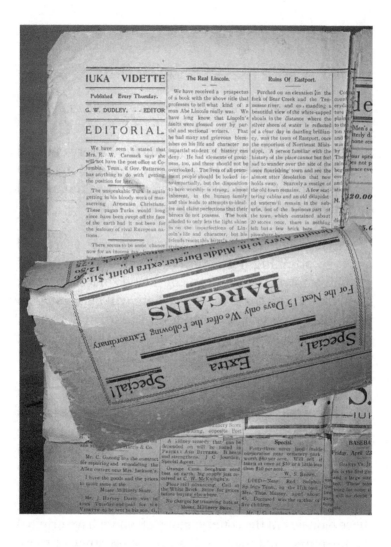

CHAPTER 10

EASTPORT CAME TO IUKA

(Excerpts from two of Miss Lyla's handwritten documents)

Years ago a very talented old lady from a very talented family was asked to write her recollections of 90 years which, when published serially in the Commercial Appeal, attracted much favorable attention.

Possessing none of the qualifications, save years, and not even attaining her length of life but with a love of my native town and being one of the two oldest citizens, I feel that in the years to come, there will be many who would like to know something of the town's history, and there will be no one to tell it. With this in mind, I will try to recall what early settlers told me and what I know to be true.

History tells us that back in the days of the Mississippi Territory, there were river settlements on the Tennessee River. Pioneers, always pushing to the west, came down the river and built homes in the wilderness years before the Treaty of Pontotoc between the Chickasaw Indians and the United States. To this day, there are descendants of those pioneers in the county, many of whom have original land patents—old maps of the U. S. show some of these pioneer settlements. Chickasaw, later renamed Riverton, lay at the mouth of Big Bear Creek, where it opens onto the Tennessee River. A settlement just across Bear Creek from Riverton later became known as Eastport.

No one knows when this settlement began, but Eastport on the Tennessee River was there in the early days of the 19th century. A stagecoach line ran from Eastport to Memphis, and many tales of heroism and tragedy are told even today of the hardships endured by pioneer travelers who came in primitive boats from their homes in the east to Eastport, where they took stages to points in Mississippi or Tennessee. One story is of a stage driver going to Memphis on one of the coldest days of winter. When the coach stopped at one of the inns, the driver did not get down; passengers began to investigate and found to their horror, the man frozen, reins still tightly held in his hands. They made every effort to revive him, with no success—unsung hero, faithful until death.

Around 1840, after a successful run of the steam engine, The Best Friend of Charleston, a movement began to build a railroad from the Mississippi River to the Atlantic Ocean. To the west, there was a short line running from Memphis to La Grange, Tennessee, and about 32 miles to the east, there was the Tuscumbia, Courtland and Decatur, with a few short lines even further east. Surveys to extend these into one continuous line prompted a movement asking towns along the way to subscribe to the effort.

This subscription effort asked Eastport for a relatively small sum, around $20,000, to have the river crossing placed there. Eastport indignantly refused. Why should Eastport, at the head of all-year navigation, with its good schools, churches and warehouses big enough to hold all the merchandise that came down the river, subscribe that much money on an untried venture? They turned the offer down, which prompted a new survey. After it was too late, Eastport tried to resend their action, but the short sight of those in authority had doomed the town. When the citizenry learned of plans to make a station eight miles to the southwest, they began as one man to destroy what they had built. They took down houses, stores and everything that had made their good town, loaded it onto big ox wagons, and took it over the Long Hungry Hollow Road to this new settlement. The beautiful city of Eastport became a memory – a place for bats and owls.

When the first contingent arrived in what would become Iuka, they found several families already there, with an established post office called Danton and a postmaster named John Robinson. This post office only lasted one year (1850 – 51).

Among the earliest settlers were the Hubbards and Usserys; they owned the land where the town grew. Colonel Cal Terry, Colonel Marcus Cook, A. T. Matthews, Dr. Benjamin Hodges and others formed a townsite company with A. T. Matthews as president. The company bought the land, and David Hubbard gave the town a block 100 feet square containing six mineral springs with the waters "forever free" to the town citizens. David Reeder Hubbard donated lands for the female academy, boarding house and Methodist Church.

The town made two surveys, the Hubbard and the Terry, and the city still uses them and their markers.

Not in the hundred years since has there been as much activity as when the townsite company held their great land sale. New townsfolk built all the old houses along Quitman Street. Eastport homeowners and merchants tore down their houses and stores to reassemble them in the new town. Only one of those houses, the William McKnight home, which stands high on the bluff on Quitman Street east, is still in existence. Just a few years ago, progress demolished the first post office/mayor's office, later known as the Carpenter House, to make way for Cutshall's Undertaking establishment. Folks are not sure which was the first house built in the new town, but the Hubbards likely built their home before the city's founding.

The Hubbard Home from Wilmer Price's Illustrated Souvenir History of Iuka found in Miss Lyla's papers.

CHAPTER 11

THE MCDONALD HOME
(Four-page account of the McDonald Home typed on
stationery with a heading marked:

McDONALD & COMPANY
T. M. McDONALD
Feed --- Seeds & Groceries
IUKA, MISSISSIPPI

Tiny holes at the top of each page indicate that they were
once held together by a straight pin.)

Much of Iuka's historical importance centers on what is known as the McDonald home, which in its prime was considered one of the town's most costly and beautiful. Although the house is nearly one hundred years old, it still attracts much attention from the traveling public. Few weeks pass that tourists, especially from the North, don't stop to see the house which so well typifies the Old South.

The McDonald Home from Wilmer Price's Illustrated Souvenir History of Iuka found in Miss Lyla's papers.

In the late 1850s when Iuka was coming into prominence with the building of the Memphis and Charleston Railroad, a childless widower, Colonel John Lawrence Moore of Huntsville, Alabama, and Memphis, Tennessee, constructed this house for his brother's family when they moved to Iuka from Gonzales, Texas. Colonel Moore also called this his home. More than fifty years ago, the McDonald family bought this house from the heirs of Colonel Moore by order of the Chancery Court for division of the heirs.

Having been an extensive traveler and possessed of wealth and good taste, Colonel Moore spared no expense in building a home that would be an addition to the new town and a joy and comfort to himself and his brother's family. As evidence of the perfect craftsmanship, the house is in good condition after nearly a century and workmen of today remark on its excellent brickwork and foundations.

The house is built of hand-planed heart pine. The walls outside are flat instead of the usual clapboard. The foundation sills are 18 inches square and put together with wooden pins instead of nails.

The house is 66 feet square, with porches or galleries on the four sides. As the builder said, "I want to have the shade in summer and follow the sun in winter." Thirty-two immense square columns support the roof, all of which are original. In fact, except for the roof and porch floors, the house is as it was built. There are six large rooms, 20 feet by 18 feet, with ceilings 16 feet high. The hall runs the entire length of the house, 12 feet wide, and all rooms open into this hall.

The house is plastered throughout, and the two parlors are hand-painted, the painting being done by an Englishman who exhibited in the English Royal Academy. This same painter, a Mr. Burton, also painted the dining room in the Gayoso Hotel in Memphis, which burned July 4, 1899. If it had not been that in years past the roof leaked on this frescoing and the fact that lightning once struck the back parlor chimney cracking the plaster, the walls would be as fresh and beautiful as when they were new.

The dining room and kitchen were originally in the basement. If that dining room could talk, many wondrous tales it could tell. Among the celebrities who have dined there are J. E. B. Stuart, General Van Dorn, Dr. Dudley Saunders, General Polk and Sterling Price of Missouri.

Tishomingo County was in the line of the contending forces during the Civil War, and Iuka was in possession of first one side and then the other. This home, being one of the best in town, was usually selected as headquarters.

Confederate General Sterling Price and his staff were domiciled here during the Battle of Iuka. General Rosecrans and his Federal forces did not completely achieve their goals at the battle because Grant failed to arrive in time with reinforcements. After the battle, Price retreated during the night, knowing if the fight continued the next day, it would be disastrous. When Grant arrived the next morning, he found the Southern army gone. Rosecrans moved into the house the Confederate general had just vacated.

Knowing the owner of the house was entirely in sympathy with the Confederates and that a son of the house was in the Confederate army, Rosecrans imprisoned the owner in the house across the street and would only let him come to his meals under guard.

With Rosecrans in possession of the town and Grant's army of 10,000 camped on the hills back of the house, a daring Confederate slipped up through the pea patch and stole some particularly beautiful horses stabled on the premises. After being caught, court-martialed, sentenced to be shot at daylight and imprisoned in a tent in the backyard, he found the sentry asleep and escaped during the night. He ran over the hills through the army encampment, reached safety at Uncle Bill Lemon's home four miles away, found a horse and rode to join his command at Holly Springs.

Another tale was that Professor George Stamps, who had been the owner and principal of the Iuka Female Institute and had joined the Confederacy under Forest, came to Iuka, procured a dilapidated buggy, disguised himself as a woman, went to Eastport where Grant's Army was encamped and sold ginger cakes to the soldiers. After gathering the needed information and maps of

Grant's Army, Mr. Stamps returned to Iuka to spend the night. He tore up a corner of the parlor carpet and hid the incriminating papers, which would have meant death to the entire household had they been found. He recovered the papers the following morning and made a safe trip to join Forrest's army, in which he was one of the most valuable spies. The carpet which sheltered those incriminating papers is still in use.

Once, as an act of derision, Federal soldiers under a Captain Harrison rode their horses all around the porch.

Today's school children hear and tell marvelous tales of the old house, such as an underground connection with the hills to the rear where soldiers escaped or tales of blood being on the walls from wounded soldiers who died in the house.

Much of the original furnishings are still in use. There's the carpet under which the papers and maps were hidden, heavy brocaded window draperies and a love seat where children of later generations have found coins from the Civil War period that indicate Federal occupancy. Among other things in the home are early telegraph instruments, Confederate money, and an early sewing machine used to make Confederate uniforms.

(Soon after Miss Lyla's death in 1962, the McDonald home was torn down.)

CHAPTER 12

LETTER FROM HATTIE...AND TOM

(Even though this appears to be a one-page handwritten letter from "Hattie" on a piece of lined stationery with a note on the back from Tom Moore beginning in mid-sentence with a "5" in the upper left-hand corner, it is probably the page five of a letter from Mr. Moore with a note on the back from Hattie.)

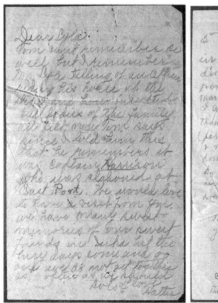
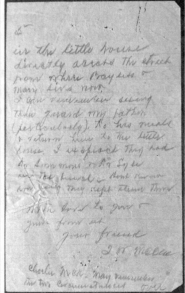

Dear Lyla

Tom can't remember so well but I remember Mrs.
Lyle telling of an officer riding his horse up the
steps and how insulted the ladies of the family
all felt, now Tom says since I told him this that
he remembers it was Captain Harrison who was
stationed at East Port. We would love to have a
visit from you. We have many sweet memories of
our sweet friends in Iuka but the busy days come
and go and we do not get together as often as we
should.

Lots of love,

Hattie

5

in the little house directly across the street from
where Bayless and Mary live now.

I can remember seeing them guard my father (particularly) to his meals and return him to the little
house. I expect they had Dr. Simmons and Dr.
Lyle in the house. Don't know how long they kept
them there.

With love to you and yours from us.

Your friend

Tom Moore

Charlie McK may remember the two circumstances.

CHAPTER 13

OTHER HISTORIC IUKA HOMES

(Contents indicate that Miss Lyla wrote this account of Iuka homes in the 1930s.)

The Old McKnight Home - Not open to the public

Entering Iuka on the Lee Highway, U. S. #72 (which through the town is Quitman Street) from the east, seated high on a bluff made by excavating this same highway, is this old home which has the distinction of having been built in two towns, Eastport and Iuka.

The house was first built in Eastport, Mississippi, by one of the early settlers of that town. The citizens of Eastport, realizing their mistake in not encouraging railroad officials to bring the line through their town, tried in vain to remedy the error, but it was too late. The exodus began, and residents moved to what became Iuka, a newly established railroad town. Comfortable homes, well-built stores, stocks of merchandise, mills, shops and everything transportable were brought over the rough mountain roads to be re-erected in the new town. This old home remains out of all the buildings brought to Iuka so long ago. The march of time has taken its toll.

The home is of no particular type of architecture, just a plain clapboard house with a porch extending across the front, two large front rooms about twenty feet square with high ceilings and massive fireplaces, two smaller rooms on a lower level and an ell. This house might go unnoticed except for the fact that it has seen the development of two towns and that one of the young sons served in Roddey's command under Forrest. The young soldier spent the end of the war in a Northern prison with the fare so meager the rats they caught for food were considered delicacies.

It is now rental property owned by J. C. Jourdan of Iuka and is in fair condition.

The Coman Home - Not open to the public

Coming into Iuka from the east over the Lee Highway, U.S. #72 (Quitman Street) at the intersection of Quitman and Court Streets, directly across from the Tishomingo County courthouse, sitting far back from the street in what has in former years been one of the most beautiful of flower gardens, is a small unpretentious cottage known locally as ROSE COTTAGE. In this modest home much of the town's history has been enacted.

Major J. M. Coman, formerly of Athens, Alabama, who came here in the town's early days by way of Eastport, Mississippi, built this house that was only half finished when he bought it. The two rooms in the yard served as living quarters and were separate from the main house while Major Coman completed construction. Logs and weather-boarding make up part of the main house, with two large front rooms separated by a wide hall. Two back rooms sit at a lower level. A back porch, which in earlier days contained a well and milk house, encloses three rooms in the wing.

The house is most unpretentious, but the flower garden during the lifetime of the original owners was the envy of the entire town with rare flowers from all parts of the country – shrubs, magnolia, mimosa and Norwegian fir trees of unusual beauty. This house also became home to John Marshall Stone, Mississippi's beloved governor.

Women gathered here during the Civil War to organize the town's first nursing association, making bandages, first aid kits and other things they gave their husbands, sons and sweethearts. Sewn within these walls was the flag of Company K, Second Mississippi Regiment, made of Iuka recruits under Captain John M. Stone. This company distinguished itself on every battlefield of Virginia in which it took part, receiving public commendation especially after the Battle of the Wilderness. General Lee himself praised Captain Stone, who had been made colonel of his regiment, for conspicuous gallantry. After the war, Colonel Stone was married in this house to the beautiful young daughter, Miss Mary G. Coman, who died only a few years ago at the advanced age of ninety.

Following the Battle of Iuka, September 19, 1862, when the town's homes were open to the wounded of both armies, many were carried to this house. Several died; some recovered. General Henry Little of Maryland died at the beginning of the battle. His body, buried in the garden, rested until after the war when his widow had it removed to Baltimore.

Many of the old slaves of this household refused freedom and lived with "Old Marse" and "Old Mistis" until their deaths, being tenderly cared for in life and given decent burials.

41

This house has always been in the family's possession. Mrs. W. B. Fulkerson, who now occupies the home, is the granddaughter.

The Hammerly Home - Not open to the public

On this same street, about two hundred yards west, at the intersection of U. S. Highway #72 (Quitman Street) and Main Street, is a white clapboard home with green blinds. The town enacted much of its religious history within these walls.

George P. Hammerly built this house in 1858-59 for his young wife in the prevailing style of old homes along this street. Houses here tell their years by their architecture, a modified Greek style. The Hammerly home remains as originally built and maintains the dignified lines some of the town's houses have lost when remodeled.

Spicy Southern cedars flank the yard, serving as a wind-break in cold weather and making an attractive sky-line when all the deciduous trees are bare.

Until a few years ago, "The Office," a separate bedroom in the yard (an old Southern custom), was the central historical point of this house. This room was known to all Southern Methodists as "The Prophet's Chamber." Like its Biblical model, a candle and pitcher of water were always at hand. No matter what hour the minister arrived, he could enter this room as freely as he would his own home and be assured of a cordial welcome when his presence was known. During the seventy-five years of its existence, this room housed the great lights of Southern Methodism - bishops, presiding elders, evangelists and laymen. It was demolished last year.

The owner of this home was the saintly George P. Hammerly, who was one of the charter members of the historic Methodist church. He brought his membership from the earlier church at Eastport, Mississippi, and became the first superintendent of the Iuka Sunday School, a position he held for more than fifty years.

A weekly Tuesday afternoon cottage prayer meeting held in this home without interruption for more than forty years, cordially welcomed the town's women and visitors. Throughout its existence, all the social activities in town gave way to this hour of prayer.

G. P. Hammerly's daughter, Mrs. Laura Copeland, keeps the home in good repair and still has a few pieces of the original furnishings.

The Matthews Home – Not open to the public

The Matthews Home from Wilmer Price's Illustrated Souvenir History of Iuka found in Miss Lyla's papers.

The Matthews home stands directly across the street from the Hammerly home, at the intersection of Main Street and U. S. Highway #72 (Quitman Street). This large, two-story Colonial home is of a more pretentious style than any other on the street and, unlike most of the homes, it faces east, with a second entrance on the north facing the highway. The reason for this, according to legend, was so the builder and president of the Iuka Townsite Company, A. T. Matthews, might have an unobstructed view of Iuka's beauty spot, The Iuka Mineral Springs Park. Later he sold off the intervening lots, and soon houses obstructed the view of the park he loved so well.

This two-story clapboard house is painted white with green blinds, and the outside chimneys are thirty feet tall. Unlike most old Southern homes, the ceilings are low, about ten feet high downstairs and less upstairs, which makes the windows very small, yet the rooms are large. There are two rooms downstairs with a hall between them. A narrow built-in staircase leads upstairs to an ell of two rooms with a porch on the north side.

Originally, in this home, as in practically all Southern homes, the kitchen and cook's room were off from the main house, connected with a covered lattice runway and a brick walkway. The kitchen and servant's room have been made into a rental apartment.

The lumber in this house is all of the best heart pine, which abounded here then. Water from nearby streams powered the mills, and the lumber was planed by hand.

Many times during the Civil War, General Forrest made this house his headquarters. A wildly excited courier came to Forrest here bearing news that two gunboats and several transports loaded to the guards with troops planned to land at Eastport on the Tennessee River eight miles away, march to Iuka, burn and sack the town, thence on to Bear Creek bridge on the Memphis and Charleston Railroad and burn the bridge thus cutting off Forrest's main army in Alabama. Forrest is said to have been lying down in the hall at the time. He received the message, called his right-hand man, Colonel D. C. Kelly, otherwise known as the Fighting Parson, and directed him to take a handful of picked men to Eastport, place cannons in advantageous positions on the bluffs and await the enemy. Such a shell fire as was never dreamed of descended on the helpless troops who fled in confusion. Two hundred drowned; seventy-five were taken prisoner. The shell fire heavily damaged the transports, Aurora and Kenton, while gunboats, the Key West and Undine, fled down the river in a panic. Confederates did not lose a man. Colonel Kelly returned to this house in Iuka with seventy-five prisoners.

After the Battle of Iuka, it was from this same home that an aged citizen, a local Methodist preacher and Justice of the Peace who was too old for military duty, went to Rosecrans army while the town was being shelled and asked for protection for the defenseless women and children. As a flag of truce, he carried a sheet nailed to a broom handle. A detachment of Rosecrans army met him, agreeing to the protection; however, Federal troops had shelled the town in the hours before, with one cannonball going through the roof of a house up the street and other homes suffering minor damage.

This house is now known as the E. N. Reed home and has never been out of the family's possession. The daughter of the original owner has preserved it well, and it contains much of the original furniture.

45

The Brown Home - Not open to the public

Facing the Lee Highway, U. S. #72, at the intersection of the highway and Pearl Street, is another house of the prevailing type of architecture seen on this street. This house attracts the eyes of the traveling public on account of the two large iron dogs that flank the stone steps.

This house was built in the boom days of the town, 1856-57-58, when Iuka promised to be a town of great business importance. Mr. James H. Doan, who became Captain James Doan of the Confederate Army, built the house.

This house is a white frame, one-story, with green blinds. A peculiarity found in so many of the old homes in Iuka is the half window placed on each side of the front window, making a double window in effect. This house has a row of tall cedars flanking the front yard. Now incorporated into the main house, the original design made the kitchen and dining room a separate building.

A stone front walk leading to the sidewalk departs from the hand-made brick walk usually seen.

This home's young husband and father joined the Confederacy during the Civil War. Soon captured for some particularly daring deed during Federal occupancy of Iuka, his captors imprisoned him in a tent in the backyard of the adjoining house used as headquarters by Rosecrans. They planned to shoot him as a spy. In vain, the wife and neighboring women begged for leniency. On the night before the execution, finding the guard asleep while still standing, the prisoner managed to escape. He slipped through the garden, where he got entangled in freshly

46

mowed peavine hay, made his way over the surrounding hills on which were encamped 10,000 enemy troops and reached the home of a farmer three miles away where he procured a fresh horse and soon regained his command. Due to this escape and for other deeds deemed hostile, Federal troops, for the rest of their occupancy, closely guarded the master of the house where Rosecrans had his headquarters.

This house is now the home of Dr. R. J. Brown and contains none of its original furniture.

The Merrill Home - Not open to the public

Directly across Quitman Street (U. S. Highway #72) from the Iuka Grammar School is another of the town's historic homes built in a modified Greek style. This home is painted cream with no blinds and no cedar trees. A distinguishing feature is the enclosed place on the roof, quaintly called "The Fish Pond." Many old homes in town had this feature, but this house alone has kept it.

After eighty years, the sound underpinning bears testament to the owners building this house of the very best lumber. Like most homes in town built about the same time, the owners made alterations. Here they changed the front porch. And originally, the design placed the kitchen and cook's room in a separate building some distance back from the main house. They replaced the roof on "The Office" a few years ago, the original being hand-drawn cedar shingles that had lasted nearly seventy years.

A cannonball went through the roof when Rosecrans shelled this house after the Battle of Iuka. The cannonball remains in possession of a nearby neighbor.

47

Several notable personalities associated with the house over the years are: the young James Fenimore Cooper, son of the distinguished novelist, and his family spent several summers here while he worked for the Memphis Appeal, Professor John Neuhardt, who helped establish the Iuka Normal Institute, called this his home and the aviator Dick Merrill, who recently made the round-trip flight to England was born here.

The daughters of the original owners dismantled the home many years ago and now manage it as a rental property.

The Howard Home - Not open to the public

Adjoining the Iuka Grammar School property on U.S. #72 is the building known as the "Old Boarding House." It was the dormitory for the first school built in the town, the Iuka Female College, established by George W. Stamps in 1856-57. A generous citizen donated the land for both the school and dormitory

The boarding house was originally much larger than it is now (another good-sized house has been made from it). It had a wide front porch supported by four square columns and a mansard roof with an observatory on the top. The roofline has changed, the observatory removed and a porch now extends across the front.

The female college flourished with its efficient corps of teachers until the Civil War began, then the president joined the Confederacy, doing valiant service oft times as a scout under Forrest. During those years, the school was suspended and not resumed until after the war. The boarding house served as a dormitory for various female colleges until 1882 when Dean and Neuhardt bought the entire female college property and established the Iuka Normal Institute. It was the first normal school south of the Mason and Dixon line. This school has served as a model for all the state teachers colleges ever since. Hundreds of young men and women received their education here in the twenty years of the school's existence. It ranked with the best in the South, and in time the founders added to the original property.

The boarding house also had its Civil War history. A line of breastworks ran through the backyard, the hills beyond being used as campsites for both blue and gray. After the battle of Iuka, the boarding house opened its doors to the wounded and dying. Grim tales of that awful day are yet told. It can truly be said of this house: "All houses wherein men have lived and died are haunted houses."

It is now private property, owned as a home by Professor S. F. Howard, but in the near future, the town will probably buy it for a much-needed high school.

The Hubbard Home - Not open to the public

The Hubbard Home from Wilmer Price's Illustrated Souvenir History of Iuka found in Miss Lyla's papers.

49

At the intersection of Lee Highway (U. S. #72) and the John M. Stone Highway (Mississippi #25) stands the oldest house in the town. It far out-dates the town's history and extends back almost as far as the county itself, making it one of the oldest, if not the oldest, in the county. Certainly, no other house in the county can boast of being owned by one family for nearly a hundred years and be in as good repair as this one.

D. R. Hubbard came to Tishomingo County from Anderson, South Carolina, soon after the county formed and built this large two-story frame house in 1840. The house faces north because when he built it, stagecoaches were the only method of transportation, and this house faced the stagecoach road, which passed through the Hubbard estate. The Memphis and Charleston Railroad paralleled the stage road through Iuka, so the house now faces the railroad.

Mr. Hubbard built his home from the best virgin timber, every foot planed by hand. The family still owns the planing tools. The floors are tongue and groove, and although they have resounded to the feet of many generations, they show minor wear. The walls and ceilings are tongue and groove pine, canvassed and papered. The front rooms are 18 feet square, and the halls both up and downstairs are 10 x 28 feet and papered in a quaint landscape pattern, admirably suited to the age of the house. Every room has a large fireplace at one end with a hand-made mantel.

Mr. Hubbard owned all the land that comprised the town of Iuka. His father and brothers came to Tishomingo County soon after the Indians left and bought up thirteen sections of land, acquiring some of it for as little as 12 ½ cents per acre. A townsite company formed once Iuka was projected, and Hubbard sold them the land, preserving his home and six acres. As a gift, he deeded the town the grounds upon which it built the Iuka Female College and dormitory. He also gave the Memphis and Charleston Railroad the land for the station and railroad right-of-way. His father deeded the Iuka Mineral Springs to the town, embracing a square of 100 feet.

Mr. Hubbard was the town's first surveyor, and his uncle was one of the early surveyors of the county. Town records show original plats consist of two surveys - the Hubbard and the Terry. Whenever a taxpayer goes to pay his taxes, he tells in which book to look.

Until a few years ago, all of the original furniture was in this home, but it has since been dismantled and is now rental property owned by the builder's daughter. The well, used until a few years ago when the town put in water works, is the original. It is about forty feet deep and has never had any form of curbing. After the Battle of Iuka, it supplied water for much of Price's army before they retreated toward Holly Springs.

The Brinkley Home - Not open to the public

The Brinkley Home from Wilmer Price's Illustrated Souvenir History of Iuka found in Miss Lyla's papers.

51

On Eastport Street, facing the Southern Railway and plainly seen from Lee Highway (U. S. #72) east, is the most beautiful of the town's old homes. DUN ROBIN, the home of the Brinkley family for many years, has more historic associations than any other spot.

Tradition says this spot is where Chief Iuka lived and where some say he is buried. A small Indian mound to the west of the house gives substance to this legend. This spot was also the home of David Hubbard, who built a log house here, and the stagecoach road passed by his front door. Colonel Marcus Cook, who was one of the members of the Iuka Townsite Company, bought this spot and, along with his sons, erected a beautiful, substantial home. Colonel Cook had a lumber mill at Cook's Landing on the Tennessee River and milled lumber for his house from timber grown on his plantation. In the early days, this house became a showplace of the town due to its location. Years later, Colonel R. C. Brinkley, one of the builders of the Memphis and Little Rock and also the Memphis and Charleston railroads, in passing through the town with his young bride, was so attracted to the place that he bought it for a summer home and gave it the name DUN ROBIN for an ancestral estate in Scotland. It has ever since belonged to the Brinkley family. Colonel Brinkley, the owner, died in 1878.

The house is of true Southern Colonial style. The immense Corinthian columns, which support the front porch, were brought from the Brinkley home in Memphis when it was demolished a few years ago. The ceiling in one room is of hand-carved walnut, with the owner's monogram in gilt in the center. The mantels are of Italian marble, and some bear the likeness of an Italian king and queen. The house has twelve rooms with a winding staircase leading to the third floor.

It was the headquarters of General Grant at one time during the Civil War, and a telegraph line ran from one of the rooms to his army's encampment at Eastport. When Grant departed, he composed a note to the owner saying he had left the property just as he found it, even the pincushion in the room. At another time, Rosecrans occupied it and had a telegraph line to his staff in the adjoining home. Confederate generals also used the home at times.

This house has a history of pestilence also. In 1878-79, when yellow fever raged in Memphis and throughout the towns of Mississippi, Iuka alone, believing so thoroughly in its healthfulness, opened its doors to the fever-stricken. They came here by the hundreds, many with the dread disease on them, many escaping. Some who came to town with the fever died, a few in the Brinkley home, but many recovered.

The Brinkley home site is on a beautiful ten-acre lot with a magnificent forest. A florist from Memphis at one time landscaped the grounds, but lately, the setting has received little attention. Two current attractions are a fine spring of mineral water and a small lake containing water lilies.

It is the home of Mrs. W. J. Brinkley and is never open to the public.

CHAPTER 14

ALMANAC FOR THE YEAR 1856 PUBLISHED BY M. A. SIMMONS, M. D. OF JACINTO

(This forty-page [a few additional pages appear to be missing at the end] Mississippi Almanac for the year 1856, published by M. A. Simmons, M. D. of Jacinto, Mississippi, is, due to age, held together by thread passing through pinholes and tied in the back. It contains extensive information on various subjects such as court calendars and monthly phases of the moon.

The last twenty pages are a discussion by Dr. Simmons about diseases of the liver, plus advertisements and 18 pages of

accolades for his Vegetable Liver Medicine and Purifying Pills. He begins his appeal and promotion with...)

TO THE PUBLIC

From the encouragement that I have had in selling, this medicine since I first offered it to the liberal and generous hearted citizens of the country, and as the public mind is so much prejudiced in its favor as to cause a great many of the most prominent citizens who were afflicted, to forsake their family physicians and put their whole trust in it, I feel that it is my duty, if it is in my power, to keep it among them. As its efficacy is now established, and I am anxious for it to maintain its character, it is the intention of the writer to enable Agents, who are not Doctors, to distinguish Liver diseases from others, and for the afflicted to read and decide for themselves, whether or not they have a Liver complaint; for although it will do good in a great many other diseases, and when used in season as a preventative, it will, by keeping the biliary and digestive organs in a healthy state, defend the system from the effects of Fever and Ague, Bilious Fever, &c. I wish to be understood, that it is only recommended as a certain and effectual remedy for Liver Complaints and diseases immediately originating from them; and as I have good and sufficient reasons to justify the belief that this Medicine will continue to spread and display its power in removing these diseases, till it may be found in almost every dwelling and doctor's shop in the known world, I will merely speak of its virtues, hoping that it may be the means of prolonging the lives of those who take it first where it has never yet been.

CHAPTER 15

IUKA METHODIST CHURCH

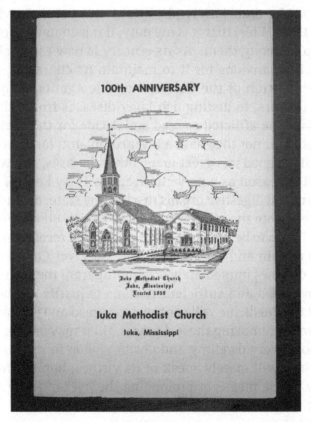

100th ANNIVERSARY

Iuka Methodist Church
Iuka, Mississippi
Erected 1859

Iuka Methodist Church

Iuka, Mississippi

(Along with a copy of the Iuka Methodist Church 100th Anniversary Centennial Program, Miss Lyla's cardboard box of papers contained two typed Iuka Methodist Church

histories, both written in the 1950s at about the same time. They are very similar. By arranging selected paragraphs from each, the two essays become one.)

In a small but thriving town in northeast Mississippi not far from the famous Muscle Shoals and Pickwick Lake, where lately the 20th Century Club received national recognition for winning the sweepstakes in the Kroger Build a Better Community Contest, there stands a Methodist Church with a history going back into the early days of the 19th century.

In the days when Mississippi and Alabama formed the Mississippi Territory nearly twenty years before the State of Mississippi joined the Union, settlements grew up at the bend of the Tennessee River, where it turned north to join the Ohio River.

Tradition, perhaps unsupported, says that De Soto, in his wanderings, first saw the Tennessee River in what is new Tishomingo County, Mississippi, and there he learned from the Indians of the greater river to the west toward which he went and discovered the Mississippi at what is now Memphis. Be that as it may, no one will ever know, but today relics surface, showing that at some point, Spaniards were here.

One of the river settlements at the mouth of Big Bear Creek took the name of Eastport and soon became a town of surprising beauty, high up on a bluff overlooking the limpid waters of the Tennessee River and the turbulent waters of Big Bear.

At the head of year-round navigation, this town was the receiving and distributing point for freight and passengers for all of northeast Mississippi. Caravans of trade came and went to distant points, and Eastport soon became the rival of Memphis on the Mississippi. There were fine homes, churches and a female college where young women learned all the arts of the day, along with Latin and Greek. Saddlers, tinners, bootmakers, a good hotel called The Mansion House, three newspapers, and a host of other trades and businesses made Eastport a town of importance. At that time, no one dreamed of other methods of transportation save river, horse, mule or the more familiar oxen.

Early in 1840, developers projected a railroad to carry traffic from the Atlantic seaboard to the Mississippi River, a continuation of many short roads already in existence in the South, among them: the Memphis and La Grange, the Tuscumbia, Courtland and Decatur, and others in Georgia, Tennessee and South Carolina. For a small sum, the developers offered Eastport the chance to be on the line. The shortsighted citizens laughed this idea to scorn. Why should untried rail transportation displace river travel? They rejected the offer, and by dismissing it, Eastport signed her own death warrant. The town was soon but a memory.

If the railroad would not come to Eastport, the town would go to the railroad. Iuka, eight miles to the southwest, was born. Eastport residents tore down their houses and took them over hills and hollows to reassemble them in the new town.

Members of both the Baptist and Methodist churches and those of the Masonic Lodge took their memberships to the new town and became charter members of Iuka's churches.

The Memphis and Charleston railroad linked together in the town of Iuka about the same time the new Iuka Methodist Church finished its construction, 1856 - 57. The early townsfolk tell many amusing tales of those days and the celebrations. One recounts an ongoing revival meeting in progress and just getting into a religious frame of mind when a steam whistle announced the arrival of a locomotive. The congregation arose and ran to see the wonderful Iron Horse. The preacher stood before empty pews, and no one returned.

The church, a substantial frame building of simple but correct proportions, had a broad porch supported by massive Corinthian columns with doors on either side leading to a long aisle extending to the pulpit. The men entered on the right side, and the women on the left, and no families sat together, a custom now long obsolete.

In the days before the Civil War, slaves worshipped seated in a broad gallery in the back that ran the full width of the building. In the afternoon, the church held Sunday school for the colored children in the main sanctuary.

War clouds that had been forming for years broke soon after the town's incorporation. Tishomingo County and Iuka suffered the ravages of both armies. They dispelled churches, burned hotels, demolished a school and carried it to Eastport to make barracks for Grant's army. Whichever army happened to possess the town at the time occupied the Methodist Church, significantly damaging it and destroying all its records.

Both armies carried their wounded and dying through the church's sacred portals following the bloody battle of Iuka. No records exist of the number who died or the countless operations and amputations made without anesthetic. Private and officer died side by side on the floor, in the pulpit, or wherever soldiers found to place a body. When the church recently made repairs, they unearthed grim relics of that frightening time.

The war suspended regular services, with local preachers occasionally filling the pulpit. Colonel Dan C. Kelly, the fighting parson and General Forrest's right-hand man, preached there when Forrest possessed the town.

At one time, when the Methodist church was seeking a location for its Southern Methodist University, Iuka asked for it, and Bishop McTeire and his committee visited Iuka to view the situation. While here, the Bishop preached powerful sermons.

Though built in 1856, 57 the church was not dedicated until more than forty years later when Bishop Hoss preached the dedication sermon.

A Statesman, a Scholar And Soldier of the Cross

BISHOP E. E. HOSS

Miss Lyla's papers contain a lengthy article from an unknown newspaper on the life of Bishop Elijah Embree Hoss (1849-1919), Southern Methodism's great "commoner."

60

The church family has remodeled and renovated the church building many times, adding to the belfry the tall spire seen from every direction when entering the town, and the church had long since removed the slave gallery. They took down the blinds and replaced the windows with beautiful cathedral glass memorials honoring the church's founders and added an apse with a handsome window depicting the Good Shepherd to honor Mr. George P. Hammerly, one of the church founders who, for more than fifty years served as superintendent of the Sunday School.

Further remodeling of the church occurred in 1934 with the addition of an educational building. The pastor at the time was the Reverend S. E. Ashmore, who directed the work to add a brick veneer and redecorate throughout. Brother Ashmore did much of the hardest work himself, and the church paid for all construction in cash. This extensive remodel greatly increased the value of the property.

It would be of interest had records been kept of all the notables who have filled the pulpit of this historic church throughout its nearly one hundred years of existence. It has resounded to the voices of many bishops, including Bishop Hoss, McTeire, Candler, and Dobbs of the Methodist faith and Bishops Hugh Miller Thompson and William Mercer Green of the Episcopal. When the body of Iuka's most illustrious citizen, Ex-Governor John Marshall Stone, was brought back for burial, the silver-tongued Bishop Charles B. Galloway pronounced the eulogy over his friend. Distinguished preachers have also filled the pulpit. When Reverend Sam P. Jones first started as an evangelist he came to Iuka. Soon the congregation overflowed the church and grew so large they had to erect a large tent in Mineral Springs Park. Such a religious awakening has never been held in Iuka before or since. Other distinguished ministers were the Reverend Sam Steele, whose Sunday articles, Creole Gumbo, were widely read and enjoyed for years, and the Reverend William McIntosh, who made his home in Iuka and sleeps his last sleep in the Iuka cemetery.

Miss Frances Willard, the founder of the Women's Christian Temperance Union and General Lew Wallace's mother, spoke in the old church.

Ministers, missionaries and other consecrated men and women have felt this church's influence and have carried forth the injunction of the Master: Go ye out into the world and preach the gospel.

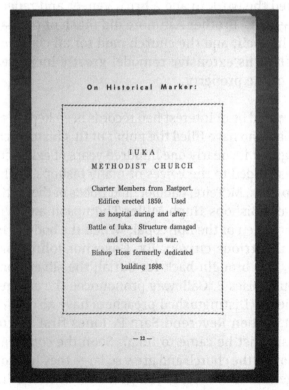

On Historical Marker:

IUKA
METHODIST CHURCH

Charter Members from Eastport.
Edifice erected 1859.   Used
as hospital during and after
Battle of Iuka. Structure damaged
and records lost in war.
Bishop Hoss formerlly dedicated
building 1898.

— 12 —

CHAPTER 16

REMINISCENCES OF GEORGE P. HAMMERLY

(This one tattered page, handwritten on the front and back by Miss Lyla with a water stain on the front, which resembles a wet glass water ring, appears to be a word-for-word interview with G. P. Hammerly which concludes with a list of Memphis Conference Preachers. The connection between these ministers and the Iuka Methodist Church is not explained. The preachers that served the Iuka church from the end of the Civil War until the late 1950s are listed in the 100th Anniversary bulletin described in Chapter 15.)

I left Athens, Alabama, in 1851, having been in school for sixteen years, was the teacher of a class of boys at Eastport for six years and came to Iuka in 1856. The Iuka Methodist Church was built in 1857-58. The old town of Eastport was broken up, and our church membership moved here. Our first preacher was Hezekiah Smith. Our Presiding Elder was M. J. Blackwell. Our second preacher was G. W. Brooks. The war came on, and we had no other preacher until 1866.

Our church was occupied by the army and all our church records lost. It was fortunate we had a church as our building was badly damaged.

This is a skip of five years covering the time of the war. A full statement would doubtless be of interest but could not be given here. I could give many instances of narrow escapes, many of which I consider providential, and it is a mercy to God I am here. I had to leave a wife and baby of six months to the tender mercies of God, but I have no regrets today for the part I took. I only regret that it was necessary.

Our company surrendered here on May 25th of 1865.

I found my family with little to eat and no fuel for fire, so I obtained a blind horse and a wagon and went on the hill where Brother Pyle now lives to get fuel.

People rallied, and we were soon a church in working order.

Our female institute was put in order, and the first Sunday school organized by Miss Donna Hill, who had reopened school. She insisted on my acting as superintendent. This continued with occasional services until our church was repaired and the coming of our new preacher who was Reverend John Barcroft and Reverend Will F. Hafford Presiding Elder.

Memphis Conference Preachers

Philip Tuggle	186- - 70
E. E. Hamilton	1871 - 72
J. D. Cameron	1873 - 74
Joseph Johnson	1875-76-77-78
J. B. Stone	1879-80-81-82
Ames Kendall	1883-84-85-86
J. B. Stone	1887-88-89
W. L. Lipscomb	1890-91-92-93

T. W. Lewis	1894
H. R. Tucker	1895-96-97-98 died '98 and
J. W. Honnell filled out term	
T. Y. Ramsey	1899
Will Young	1900-1901-1902-03
W. C. Harris	1904-1905-06-07
B. P. Jaco	1908-9-10-11
J. H. Mitchell	1912-13-14-15
T. H. Dorsey	1916-19

PASTORS

According to records, the following pastors served the
Iuka Methodist church after the Civil War:

Rev. John Barcroft	Rev. P. E. Duncan
Rev. A. L. Pritchard	Rev. J. D. Cameron
Rev. R. L. Harper	Rev. T. H. Lipscomb
Rev. J. E. Douglas	Rev. O. L. Savage
Rev. J. C. Lowe	Rev. J. B. Randolph
Rev. J. M. Boone	Rev. W. L. Graves
Rev. Thomas S. Campbell	Rev. C. P. Moss
Rev. J. H. Scruggs	Rev. W. D. McCullough
Rev. J. F. Markham	Rev. L. A. McKeown
Rev. W. H. Armstrong	Rev. H. E. Carter
Rev. J. R. Robinson	Rev. Walter W. Jones
Rev. J. B. Johnson	Rev. G. C. Schwartz
Rev. J. H. Mitchell	Rev. E. M. Shaw
Rev. G. W. Gordon	Rev. S. E. Ashmore
Rev. D. L. Cogdell	Rev. W. H. Mounger
Rev. John W. Bell	Rev. E. G. Mohler
Rev. W. C. Harris	Rev. J. H. Holder
Rev. W. W. Woollard	Rev C. W. Avery
Rev. Thomas Cameron	Rev. W. V. Stokes
Rev. J. H. Shumaker	Rev. G. R. Meaders
Rev. H. T. Gains	Rev. R. E. Wasson
Rev. R. M. Davis	Rev. J. T. McCafferty, Jr.

CHAPTER 17

COPIED FROM MISS ANNA LOU'S
DIARY – 1857 to 1882

(With no indication as to the identity of Miss Anna Lou, Miss Lyla copied, by hand, TWO almost identical, two-page excerpts from her diary. They give a glimpse into early Iuka's downtown and surrounding area.

Miss Anna Lou may be Anna Lou Matthews Reed, daughter of A. T. Matthews, one of Iuka's founding fathers. Anna Lou Reed lived a couple of houses down the street from Miss Lyla.

Also, it is worthy of note that none of the businesses along Fulton and Front streets in downtown Iuka survived a massive fire in March 1896.

Be patient with Miss Anna Lou's diary and give her people, places and hundred-year-old descriptions time to unravel. You may find a nice, long-lost picture of Iuka painted between the lines.)

Business Square – East side facing west nearest R. R. on corner – south to north

Hart & Powell – Dean & DeWoody – P. O. Mrs. Heathman Post Mistress – Mrs. J. D. James millinery – Dr. Payne drug store – Bates & Burgess – Ellis & Neblett – books – J. H. Doan

North side facing south – east to west
Corner Hammerly & Price – Mrs. Jack Moore – Dr.
M. A. Simmons.

**Continuing west across Main Street – north facing
south**
A. T. Matthews corner – Moore – J. B. McKinney

South of the railroad near the creek
Dan Coleman – Thompson Livery Stable – Collier's
shop – Presbyterian Church – Henry Krause Furniture store

*(The diary did not mention if the statement above is east
to west or west to east, but reports in other articles and
pamphlets suggest that it is probably east to west.)*

--

After the Memphis and Charleston Railroad, the first
settlers moved here from Eastport, one or two
houses being torn down and rebuilt here. One I know
belonging to Mr. William McKnight.

South of the railroad were the first building lots chosen.

East of the creek running north and south, Marcus
Cook, father of Frank, Jim, Mrs. John McKnight and Mrs.
Billy Nolen, built the house now known as the Brinkley
place. Colonel R. C. Brinkley bought this after the war,
the Cooks having left here.

Colonel Cal Terry's home was east of the Cook place,
and after the war, it was sold to Mrs. Scudder, sister of
Mr. Brinkley. Afterwards, it sold to Mrs. Bowers, who
had daughters Lula and Gillie. Mr. or Mrs. Bowers sold
to the Crenshaws, and Mr. Crenshaw sold to B. F. McRae.

Both Cook and Terry places were north of the railroad. *[McRae sold to the Van Eatons, and, at the last, the place was known as the Ad Foote place. It burned in 1896 or 97.]*

South of the railroad, Dr. Ben Hodges built opposite the Cook home. Later that house burned. Mr. W. J. Hart bought the lot and built the house which now stands there in 1866. Mrs. Hart sold the place to Mrs. R. H. Allen when the Harts moved to Texas in 1882.

Across the road south was Mr. William McKnight's home moved here from Eastport. Mr. Emmet Reno, brother-in-law of Sam, Will and Miss Tony DeWoody, built back of the McKnight place now known as the W. B. Ellis home. The Reno girls were Lula, Birdie and Minnie. This home was built after 1866. Mr. W. G. Stainback, I suppose, later bought this place from Mr. Reno and had charge of the male academy while living here. He later returned to Inverness, Mississippi. Mrs. Stainback was related to Mrs. Harris and Miss Mollie Lawrence, and Mrs. Harris lived first in this Reno-Stainback home. She later bought the place on the creek facing the Park, which was owned by the Bates.

Mrs. Bates was a sister to Mr. Burgess. I don't know who built this house, but Mrs. Bates sold to a Mr. Shelton, who had two little girls, Allie and Frankie. The Sheltons sold it to Mrs. Harris, who afterwards sold it to Mr. C. W. McKnight.

The Bates moved to a home further up the hill. Knox Bates died of yellow fever. Allie Bates married Jim Dugger. This house was built by Colonel Wisdon, who married Miss Anna Terry. The Wisdons lived here for several years then returned to Jackson, Tennessee.

This house was near the Saddlers, Dr. Sawyer and Mr. Fussell. A Mrs. Burt lived in the Saddler home. She had a little daughter named Katy. Afterwards the Steeles lived there, Dr. Sam and Miss Julia who married Reverend E. B Ramsey.

Copied from Miss Anna Lou's diary.

Iuka in 1857 up to 1882.

Business square. East side facing west nearest R.R. on corner, Hart & Powell. Dean & Dewoody. P.O. Mrs. Heathman. Mrs. J. D. James millinery. Dr. Payne drug store. Bates & Burgers - Ellis & Neblett - books - J. H. Doan.

North street facing south. Corner Hammerly & Price. Mrs. Jack Moore - Dr. M. A. Simmons. across street W. F. Matthews corner. Moore. J. B. McKinney -

South of the R.R. near the creek Dan Coleman - Thompson Livery stable - Collier shop Presbyterian church. Henry Krause Furniture store.

After the Memphis & Charleston R.R. the first settlers moved here from Eastport - one or two houses being torn down & rebuilt here - one I know belonging to Mrs. Wm. McKnight. South of the railroad the first building lots chosen.

East of the creek running north & south - Lanier running Marcus Cook. Father of Frank - Jim, Mrs. John McKnight Mrs. Billy Nolen - the house now known as the Brinkley place. Col. R. C. Brinkley bought this after the war. The Cooks having left here.

Col. Cal Terry's home east of the Cook place & after the war was sold to Mrs. Scudder, sister of Mrs. Brinkley afterwards sold to Mrs. Bowers who had two daughters Lillie Lula & Billie Bowers. Mollie Bowers married Bob Marshall Dave Bowers married Marcella Bates. Mrs. Bowers sold to the Crenshaw & Mr. Crenshaw sold to B. H. McRae, McRae sold to Van Eatons & at the first the place was known as

CHAPTER 18

MEMPHIS AND CHARLESTON RAILROAD

*(This handwritten excerpt comes from one of Miss Lyla's
lengthy narratives on the history of Iuka.)*

The Memphis and Charleston was the outgrowth of
many shorter, previously existing roads. Some of
them, like the South Carolina Railroad and the Tuscumbia
Railroad, both constructed in 1830, were among the first
lines built in the United States. The original Tuscumbia
Railroad only ran a few miles from Tuscumbia to Tuscumbia
Landing, but with slave labor, Colonel Sherrod, a wealthy
Tennessee River Valley planter, extended the line about
sixty miles into the Tuscumbia, Courtland and Decatur
Railroad. This construction pauperized the once-
wealthy landowner.

The LaGrange and Memphis Road also went into the
construction of the Memphis and Charleston. La Grange
was, at that time, an important town in west Tennessee,
a town of wealth and culture. The building of this road
was the dream of General E. P. Gaines, who died ten
years before it was built.

March 27, 1857, in Iuka, a grand celebration announced
the coming together of the Memphis and Charleston
Railroad from the east and the west with a golden spike

to mark the spot. A particular high official was to have the honor of completing the road, but when the time came for him to drive the spike, he had unfortunately looked too often upon the wine when it was red, and after several ineffective attempts to hit the head, he turned to a ditch digger standing by and said, "Pat can you hit that d- spike?"

Pat replied, "Faith and begorry, I'm the very man who can." To Pat O'Leary fell the honor of completing the Memphis and Charleston Railroad.

The celebration continued in the Spring Park with a picnic and balloon ascension. After the festivities, a free train trip of a few miles was offered to anyone willing to risk life and limb on such a hazardous venture, and a few daring souls accepted. Many amusing but true tales have come down through the years of this momentous occasion. One of the women had left her bread to rise, and when the train was about two miles out of town, she screamed, "Oh, my bread will run all over the floor." She grabbed the bell cord, jumped from the train and ran two miles back to town to save her precious bread.

The Baptist Church, which was the first church built in town, was on the south side where Mr. W. A. Jourdan's home now stands. A revival was in progress, but when the whistle of the first locomotive was heard, religious fervor gave way to curiosity. With one accord, the whole congregation ran out of the church, leaving the preacher in the pulpit with one zealous couple in a pew alone. Closing his Bible, the preacher remarked, "Well, I reckon we might as well go too." They did.

After the lines joined up here in Iuka, the celebration continued in Memphis, where grand speeches fancifully proclaimed The Marriage of the Waters with a barrel of ocean water being poured into the Mississippi River.

John Marshall Stone became Iuka's first depot agent for the new railroad in Iuka, with McPeters as the telegraph operator. In the 100 years of the railroad's existence, there have been only four agents: John Marshall Stone, Edwin Merrill, Berry Martin and C. R. McCulley.

Memphis & Charleston Railroad freight charge receipt written on February 4, 1861 to J. L Moore for items that totaled $24.33. The station agent, J. M. Stone, signed the receipt.

The building of the railroad opened a new era in the county, but as with all innovations, some decried the program. There were many lawsuits brought against the railroad for cattle-killing. One woman, after several of her cows were caught on the right of way, armed herself with a bucket of soft soap. She poured it on the rails. The wheels of the Iron Horse lost traction and spun ferociously, giving her cows ample time to get off. She was detected and admonished for her efforts but not arrested.

With the coming of the railroad, thoughts turned to education. Most of the populace who had come from Eastport were cultured, educated people and had provided good schools in Eastport and were anxious for their children to have opportunities equally as good here. Under the direction of a northern man named Professor Norcum, a boy's Military Academy was built east of the Spring Park, about where one of the colored churches now stands. Professor George Stamps, who came from the Marshall Institute in Marshall County near Holly Springs, established The Iuka Female Academy, where the school now stands. Professor Stamps brought a full core of teachers trained in all the arts and graces of that day. There were several boarding pupils also with the boarding house adjoining the school.

Among the earliest settlers to the town, we find the names of Coman, Collier, Dean, Davis, Blythe, Anderson, Eccles, Hammerly, Barnett, Chism, James, Hodges, Lyle, Weaver, Moore, McKnight, Doan, Matthews, Cayce, McIntosh, Cox, Settle, Coleman, Thompson, Ussery and Stamps.

After the completion of the railroad, the place grew rapidly. By December 1857, it became an incorporated town with Demonthenes L. Davis elected as the first mayor and Tom Weaver as the marshal. Davis was popular with many talents and abilities. He was the first postmaster, a newspaperman, a local preacher and a portrait painter of some ability. It is not known where he lived nor where he went from here. The first post office was in a frame building on the west side of the town square, about where Cutshall's Furniture Store is now. Davis was also the first editor. His newspaper was strangely named The Mink.

The Blythe Hotel was soon built, occupying the same spot as today's Leatherwood Hotel, which is the third hotel on that same spot. J. J. Blythe was the second postmaster, and he moved the post office to the hotel.

CHAPTER 19

IUKA FEMALE INSTITUTE
PHOTOS AND STUDENTS IN 1859 – 1860

*(The following photographs of the Iuka Female Institute
and its Dormitory are from an unidentified and undated
newspaper clipping found in Miss Lyla's four-page
"scrapbook" that is described in more detail in Chapter 44.)*

IUKA FEMALE INSTITUTE

*(The caption with this photograph says: THE FIRST SCHOOL
BUILDING erected in Iuka, Mississippi, in 1856–57...the Iuka
Female College under Professor George Stamps. During
the Civil War it was used as a hospital and morgue for*

74

the wounded and the slain of both the Federal and the Confederate armies following the battle of Iuka. Later this building housed the Iuka Normal Institute, said to be the first Normal in the South.)

IUKA FEMALE INSTITUTE DORMITORY

(The caption reads: WHERE BOARDING STUDENTS of Iuka Female College were housed in 1856-57. This is also one of the very first buildings erected in Iuka. It has much Civil War history, and afterwards became the dormitory for Iuka Normal Institute and was used for more than twenty years.)

(The following partial list of IFI students from 1859 – 1860 handwritten on the backs of two WPA [Works Progress Administration] Individual Manuscript Forms from 1936, brings with it some questions. It would be interesting to know where Miss Lyla got the names because of the additional data like marital status and spouse name. It was almost certainly compiled after 1860. What was the occasion? Reunion?)

75

(The list of students appears incomplete probably by a couple of pages because it is alphabetical with blocks of letters [D – M and S – Z] missing. Those who did make the list are among the first students of the Iuka Female Institute.)

Bettie McIntosh — Dan Enderson
Laura J. McIntosh · Mr. Hyatt
Mattie McIntosh
Nattie McIntosh
Linda J. McKnight — J. B. McKinneY
Mattie McP
Annie McKinney
Nannie McCrummon, Col. Dowd —   Smithville
Alice McCrummon
Maggie McCorkle   Henderson Co. Tenn.
Sallie
Alice Mann   Martin Williams   Allatona Ala.
Florence Matthews   Q. Castleberry
Nattie Meek   Mr. Mary
Lizzie Moulton   W. Belue
Sarah Morris
Mary T. Price   Capt. Hyatt
Mattie Purdy   O'Neil
Mary Eliza Prichett
Isabella Richardson   Panola Co. Miss.
Helen Ross   Henderson Co. Tenn.
Lethe Smith   Cherokee Ala.
Florence Smith
Josie Stamps
Sue Sargent
Bettie Settle   Jno. Williams

(For a complete typed list of these students plus their places of residence and other data, see the APPENDIX – Chapter 19 Excerpt.)

77

CHAPTER 20

WAR CLOUDS

(Handwritten account from the same document as Chapter 18)

Almost as soon as the town was incorporated, yea even before the town was dreamed of, war clouds were gathering. By 1858 a census in Tishomingo County was made to ascertain how many men were of military age.

In 1860, a secession convention was held in Jackson. Tishomingo County representatives voted against secession but were outvoted by hotter heads, so when South Carolina seceded, Mississippi soon followed.

The Civil War history of Tishomingo County, which at that time embraced Alcorn and Prentiss, is endless. Being in the line of contending forces, each one anxious for means of transportation by both the Tennessee River and the Memphis and Charleston Railroad, battles were fought at Eastport, Iuka, Burnt Mills, Shallow Wells (or Belmont), Corinth, Farmington, Brice's Cross Roads, Blackland, Rienzi and Bear Creek Bridge.

CHAPTER 21

SKIRMISH AT BEAR CREEK BRIDGE

(This article is handwritten on the same large piece of paper as the Recollections of Eastport in Chapter 7 and Ruins of Eastport in Chapter 9.)

Bear Creek Bridge on the Southern Railroad

On the morning of April 13, 1862, just one week after the sanguinary contest at Shiloh, a sleepy Confederate picket at Chickasaw (now Riverton on the Tennessee River, ten miles northeast of Iuka) was awakened by the chug-chug of a gunboat descending the river. Peering through the dim, foggy atmosphere, he could discern the light of a lantern on the front deck of the approaching boat. He spurred his horse to where his comrades were asleep nearby and called sharply to wake them. By the time they had mounted, the gunboat was getting quite near. The Confederate cavalrymen fell back a safe distance and watched developments. They soon saw another, which was followed by two transports, the deck of the latter blue with soldiers. The two gunboats came to anchor, one on each side of the landing, while the transports steamed to the shore, threw out gang planks and began landing troops. The Confederates saw a troop of cavalry, three infantry regiments and a battery of artillery come ashore. Quickly forming, cavalry in advance, the Federals started up the Bear Creek Valley Road. The Confederates fell back before them, having previously sent a courier to Iuka where about 100 men (members of the 2nd Tenn. Cavalry) were encamped. The squad of Confederates fell back to the old Free Bridge. There they crossed to the west side of Bear Creek, firing the bridge behind them. Waiting only long enough to see that the bridge was well on fire, they galloped on by the nearest route to Bear Creek railroad bridge, feeling sure that the federals, who were under command of General W. T. Sherman, were detailed for the express purpose of destroying this bridge. When they reached the close vicinity of the bridge, they overtook their comrades who had come from Iuka. These troops, whose entire force did not exceed 150, dismounted and stationed themselves along the bluff and in the thick timber near the west end of the bridge to defend it from destruction. Scarcely had they got in position before the enemy approached on the other side. A sharp skirmish ensured for a few minutes, but the Federals were in such overwhelming force besides being armed with long-range guns that the Confederates soon retired, leaving the bridge to its fate. The ascending columns of smoke soon showed the work of destruction was now on. As soon as the bridge was sufficiently consumed to render its destruction certain, the Federals returned to Chickasaw, re-embarked and returned down the river.

The present bridge was constructed only a few years since and is a handsome, substantial structure. Vidette May 13, 1909

CHAPTER 22

FAIRFAX WASHINGTON AND
SHALLOW WELLS

*(This one folded page of extremely fragile paper with
handwriting on the front and back has missing fragments
that took several words and phrases. Underlined
replacements complete the sentences.)*

I<u>n a simple</u> but plainly marked <u>grave</u> in Oak Grove
Cemetery <u>lies the</u> remains of Fairfax Washington,
great-nephew of George Washington. Until recently, no
one knew anything of the history of the young soldier
buried on the lot of one of Iuka's earliest and most
prominent families - the McKnight family.

Early, most casual inquiries only brought to light that
Fairfax Washington was a young soldier in the Confederate
army who possibly died of wounds in the McKnight home.
Now in these later years, all members who would have
been able to tell more details are dead.

According to the letter I received years ago from a
Gulfport, Mississippi, citizen who said she had lived as a
neighbor to the Washington family, Fairfax was the son
of Fairfax Washington, Sr., who moved to Handsboro,
Mississippi, from Virginia in the early 1840s. After moving
to the Mississippi Gulf Coast, he (Fairfax Washington

Sr.) was soon married to Sarah Richards, whose family he had known in Virginia and had moved to Mississippi earlier. Fairfax Washington Jr. was one of several children born into this marriage. His three brothers were Richard Warner, Dr. John Washington and Reade. His sisters were Lou, who married a Dr. Bell, a Presbyterian Minister, Sally and Betty. Betty was never married and lived on the Gulf Coast until a few years ago. Reade, the youngest of the children, is old, feeble and in his 80s.

The Washingtons brought to the new home in Mississippi many family heirlooms such as a rosewood piano, family silver, mahogany furniture and other precious treasures. They were said to have lived up to all the best of the family traditions.

Young Fairfax Washington enlisted in the Confederacy when a mere child. According to the information given to the writer by Mrs. Walsh of Gulfport, who knew the family well, two young cousins joined a Louisiana regiment.

One was, according to the tombstone record, Fairfax. He was only 14 when he died. The other was Edward Washington Butler Jr., the son of Major George Washington Butler and Frances Parke Lewis, great-granddaughter of Martha Washington. By a strange coincidence, both boys were killed in the Battle of Shallow Wells in Tishomingo County, Mississippi, or were wounded and died of wounds. After the lapse of so many years, no one can give accurate information.

CHAPTER 23

IUKA AND STREIGHT'S RAID

(Miss Lyla handwrote ten pages about Streight's Raid, a well-documented Civil War engagement with origins in and about Tishomingo County, Mississippi. The first five of her pages are included here in Chapter 23. She did not indicate the source of her information except for a reference on Page 5 to Jordan's __Campaigns of Forrest__.)

Streight's Raid in 3 installments. Number 1 - April 23, 1896.

Many of our readers have heard of Streight's Raid, and quite a number of them who are Ex-Confederates took part in the pursuit. It was one of the most brilliant, romantic and dashing episodes of the Civil War, and it established a solid foundation for all time the fame of Bedford Forrest and his gallant cavalry troops.

On the 23rd of April 1863, General Forrest received orders from General Bragg to move swiftly from Spring Hill, Tennessee, to Decatur, Alabama, and give relief to General Roddey. Roddey was hard-pressed and greatly outmatched by a column of Federal infantry marching under General Dodge from Corinth to Tuscumbia accompanied by 2,500 picketed cavalry. They had landed at Eastport under Colonel Streight and joined Dodge near Iuka.

Roddey's command camped at the Mhoon farm between Cherokee Station and the Tennessee River.

Roddey had heard rumors of the approaching column, and on the 22nd of April, he dispatched Sergeant J. B. McKinney, now a citizen of Iuka, with three men as scouts to report the force and movements of the enemy. The three men were Newman Cayce, now judge of the judicial district, Dabney Ray and John Hill.

These scouts first proceeded to Stemini Ferry above the railroad. Here they learned from a woman that a company of Federal cavalry had just left on the west side of the creek. They thought it prudent both to wait till morning and cross below the railroad. This they did, traveling in an old skiff, leaving their horses hitched in the swamp. Advancing continuously through the woods, they reached the summit of a high hill just beyond the crest of which they came upon two Federal videttes who started to charge the scouts but turned and ran.

The scouts discovered the enemy encamped with a heavy force of infantry and cavalry at the Marcus Cook Farm about one mile west of Bear Creek. After getting all the information available, the scouts hastily recrossed Bear Creek and conveyed words to Roddey's men.

That morning, the 23rd, Julian's battalion of Roddey's command had been sent out on the Iuka and Tuscumbia Road in the direction of Stemini Ferry. A regiment of Federal cavalry had crossed with two pieces of artillery and were advancing toward Tuscumbia. Julian's battery struck this column and, after a faint skirmish, fled precipitously toward Tuscumbia.

General Roddey had broken camp in the morning as soon as he heard the report of his scouts and hurried southward across the railroad, striking the Tuscumbia Road at Newsom's Farm. Just as the head of the column struck the road, the two pieces of artillery yet in sight had passed eastward while the Federal cavalry regiment had, as learned later, already reached Barton station and were feeding their horses.

The section of Federal artillery was supported by about 60 infantry as dismounted cavalry and, as soon as they perceived Roddey's command, hastened to the top of an eminence at Calvin Goodloe's place and unlimbered for action.

General Roddey called on the head of the company to charge the battery, but as they did not respond promptly, he called up Company 1 from the rear of his old regiment, commanded that day by Captain J. R. Williams, a brother of John W. Williams of Iuka.

This company, quickly forming, charged straight ahead, capturing the battery and the support. One Dutchman driving a caisson escaped in the direction of Barton but was captured by two of the company, McKinney and Weaver, in sight of the Federal regiment. This regiment remounted and returned to the place of conflict. In the meantime, Federal infantry in considerable force had formed a line of battle to the north of the road in an open field in Roddey's rear.

Roddey's command had also formed a line on the same side of the road.

The Federal cavalry regiment returning from Barton organized into platoons and broke thru the Confederate's cavalry after a desperate hand-to-hand conflict in which they lost several men and rejoined the Federal infantry. General Roddey fell back south of Barton carrying one piece of the captured artillery and one caisson, disabling the other and throwing it into a railroad cut.

The Federals pursued their course towards Tuscumbia after halting for their forces to come up.

General Roddey whiffed around again and came to their front near Tuscumbia.

The next day, Friday Apr. 24, the Federal column reached Tuscumbia. General Roddey's command retired eastward where four miles from Tuscumbia they were joined by the 11th Tennessee, 600 strong of Forrest's command, which had crossed the Tennessee River that morning.

Roddey's men continued to fall back, skirmishing as they went, finally crossing to the east side of Town Creek. In describing the following events, we draw mainly from Jordan's <u>Campaigns of Forrest</u>.

On the night of the 27th, they were joined by General Forrest with three more regiments. That astute commander had already, it seems, divined that the main object of the Federal expedition was to send a cavalry raid through north Alabama and north Georgia and destroy the Confederate ships and factories at Montevallo and Rome. Believing that General Dodge's infantry command had come along merely to support and cover the cavalry movement until the latter got well on their way, General Forrest had sent two regiments to Florence to threaten the Federal rear.

On the morning of April 28, he made ready at an early hour for the Battle of Town Creek. He posted two of his regiments south of the Tuscumbia Road with their right resting on the road while Roddey's command was placed to the left to watch the upper crossing known as Shallow Ford which was not very shallow at that particular time owing to recent heavy rains....

(This conflict continued for days moving east. Eventually, Forrest captured Streight's entire army at Cedar Bluff, Alabama, on May 3rd.)

CHAPTER 24

BATTLE OF EASTPORT

(This description of the Battle of Eastport comes from an incomplete, typed narrative on the history of Iuka and the surrounding area that begins on a Page 3 and ends on a Page 12. Miss Lyla wrote it before Pickwick Dam's completion in the 1930s. Tiny holes at the top of each page indicate they were once held together by a straight pin.)

With the completion of the Memphis and Charleston Railroad in 1857, the town of Eastport was demolished. Homes and stores were torn down and brought to the new town of Iuka, where they were rebuilt. In a few years, Eastport became naught but a memory.

With the filling of Pickwick Lake, even the town site will be obliterated.

A critical battle was fought there in 1864 when a small company of Confederates under the command of Colonel D. C. Kelly of Forrest's army quietly stationed themselves in the hills overlooking the river. Two Federal gunboats, the Key West and Undine, and several transports steamed up the river on a mission to land troops at Eastport, march to Bear Creek bridge on the Memphis and Charleston Railroad eight miles away and burn it. After the soldiers disembarked, a terrific cannonading took place. Two hundred Federals drowned, seventy-five taken prisoner, and two of the transports, the Aurora and Kenton, were set fire and heavily damaged by shell fire. The gunboats and remaining troops put down the river.

Many tales are still told of the fierce encounter.

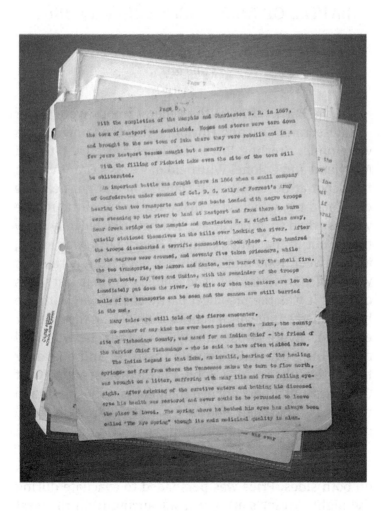

CHAPTER 25

BATTLE OF IUKA – SEPTEMBER 19, 1862

(Handwritten excerpt from the same document as Chapters 18 and 20)

In the Battle of Iuka, the Federal troops were under Rosecrans, Ord and Hurlbut while the Confederates were under Sterling Price of Missouri, Henry Little of Maryland and Colonel Whitfield of Texas. Grant was in the depot at Burnsville and claimed he did not hear the cannonading, which was fierce for hours, although he was less than six miles away. The battle lasted only a few hours, but in that time, General Henry Little was killed, and between 1000 and 1500 brave boys from both sides were killed or wounded. Old soldiers in their last years claimed it was the bloodiest battle of the war, with the highest percentage of casualties considering the number engaged. Every house in town cared for the wounded and dying. The Iuka Female Institute and boarding house, the Iuka Springs Hotel, the Methodist and Baptist Churches and others opened their doors as hospitals and morgues. Older men who were small children then told of the screams without anything to alleviate the agony.

With his troops exhausted and the death toll tremendous on both sides, Price was persuaded to evacuate during the night. Grant's army was advancing from the west with fresh troops, and Price's advisers pointed out that all the odds were against him. When Grant arrived the following morning, he was surprised to find Rosecrans in command and Price's army on the march to meet Van Dorn at Holly Springs.

In his pamphlet of the Battle of Iuka, Confederate soldier G. W. Dudley, who came to Iuka in the late 1890s and edited the Iuka Vidette, gives the battle in its entirety. This was copied in a short history of Iuka published in 1924.

The town was almost devastated. The Blythe Hotel burned, and many private homes were damaged. Cannonballs went through the roofs of both the house across from the Iuka Female Institute and the Iuka Springs Hotel. The Methodist Church was severely damaged, and all church records were destroyed. General Henry Little of Maryland was killed at the beginning of the battle as he rode up to deliver a message to General Sterling Price. Colonel Celsus Price caught him as he fell from his horse. General Little was buried in the garden of Major James Coman. After the war, his widow came from Baltimore and had his remains taken there for permanent burial.

The Federal dead, who were buried on the hills, in the schoolyard, and on grounds around the hotel and churches, were disinterred after the war and carried to Corinth for burial in the National Cemetery. The Confederates were buried in a trench in Shady Grove Cemetery. Years after the war, members of the John Marshall Stone chapter of the U. D. C. sponsored a tribute, and the citizens of Missouri and Texas (the troops engaged in the battle) made it possible by erecting a handsome monument to mark the sacred spot. Due to the site's remoteness, the traveling public seldom saw it, so the town moved it to the courthouse yard.

Photo of "Relics from the Battle of Iuka," from Wilmer Price's Illustrated Souvenir History of Iuka found in Miss Lyla's papers.

CHAPTER 26

RECOLLECTIONS OF A SOLDIER
IN THE BATTLE OF IUKA

(This account written by Miss Lyla on brittle paper does not give a source.)

I stood in the road with my company in front of the Rick's home, and General Rosecrans and his staff came up from the rear, the first time we had seen him that day. My regiment was in advance. The man who was struck with the flat of his sword was a private of Company A of my regiment named Tubbo, who was wounded during the battle but lived through the war. Rosecrans struck him because he had been in the house. The panic Miss Williams spoke of was in the rear of our lines and was the falling back of the regiment that was placed in the rear of our line and could not fire but was under fire, losing men.

I saw nothing of what was happening in the rear as my regiment was first under fire. We were the only regiment on the right side of the battery and almost at right angles to it. We had all we could attend to in the front. We lost more than any other regiment in the battle. My company (B) lost 28 men out of 60, killed and wounded. We held our position until dark, and being out of ammunition, we retired to the field southeast of the Rick's home for ammunition, and the 11th Missouri took our place. The Confederates were occupying the ridge just back or west of our position. I was in the ravine between the two lines when the Confederate's fired their first volley but could not see them for the smoke and darkness but saw their line of fire and got through the line of Missouri boys before they opened fire. As I passed through, an officer complimented us by saying we had done "splendid."

The battery lost more men than any other battery in the war in a single engagement. They were in a heavy crossfire. Their position was in the northeast angle of our line of battle so that they received the Confederates fire from the east and the north of the Missouri companies. It was the hardest fight I was in, and I never saw a union or a Confederate soldier who was there who didn't say the same thing.

J. Q. A. Campbell
Bellefontaine Ohio

CHAPTER 27

AFTER THE WAR

(Four paragraphs from two of Miss Lyla's documents – one handwritten, one typed – that show how quickly Iuka sprang back to life after the Civil War)

After the war, the Female Institute, which had flourished under Professor George Stamps, resumed, and the people took up the burden of life again. They rebuilt the railroad, and Colonel John M. Stone, who had commanded a regiment and won glory on many a battlefield of northern Virginia, was once again the depot agent. Colonel Stone resigned later to be state senator from Tishomingo County and went to the governorship after the infamous Adelbert Ames left office under fire.

Iuka was in its heyday in the 70s. A fine hotel, The Mineral Springs Hotel, replaced the red-framed Iuka Springs Hotel, which burned in 1869. Summer boarders so soon filled the rooms that the hotel added an annex at once. It had the finest ballroom between Memphis and Chattanooga, an orchestra playing for meals, and mighty dances. To attend the opening ball was considered an honor, and the wealth and beauty of the South gathered there. In those days, Iuka bid fair to compete with White Sulphur Springs, Virginia. Everyone's home was open to boarders, and from 500 to 1000 visitors spent the summers here. The fame of the water went all over the South.

The buildings of the Female Institute were used by successive schools as dormitory and school, among others, by Dr. Douglass from the La Grange Academy and Professors Pettus and Flournoy, who established the Iuka Male and Female Academy. Under Pettus and Flournoy, the Female school resided in these buildings, and the Male Academy was on the north side of town. Professor Pettus was a near relative of Senator Pettus of Alabama.

In 1882 the Iuka Male and Female Institutes merged into the Iuka Normal Institute. Founders H. A. Dean and John Neuhardt were Lebanon Ohio Normal College graduates. They also had degrees from other colleges. This school flourished for 20 years, during which it furnished teachers, physicians, surgeons, lawyers, members of Congress, and U. S. senators to the entire South. One could hardly go in any direction without meeting graduates from the Iuka Normal Institute. All the teachers colleges and normals over the South patterned themselves after that school, and it flourished for 20 years, closing its doors on February 1, 1902.

CHAPTER 28

STUDENTS AND TEACHERS AT THE IUKA
FEMALE INSTITUTE IN OCTOBER 1870

(On what is now one sheet of fragile paper, Miss Lyla carefully handwrote in ink the names of students and teachers at the Iuka Female Institute in 1870. The first names of several students are missing due to ragged edges. For the complete list of 75 students, see the APPENDIX – Chapter 28 Excerpt.

The founder of the Institute, George Stamps, is not listed as part of the school's administration in 1870. The new staff is:)

Rev. J. E. Douglass – President and Professor of Moral & Mental Sciences - Ancient languages
Bettie Hunt – Math – French – Natl. Phil – Astronomy Ancient History – Art Dept.
Mrs. E. A. Neblett   Rhetoric – Philosophy – Botany History U. S. Gov. and Eng Literature
Mrs. F. E. Steger – Music
Miss L. A. DeWoody – Preparatory Dept.

CHAPTER 29

CATALOGUE FOR THE IUKA FEMALE INSTITUTE SCHOOL YEAR ENDING JUNE 16, 1875

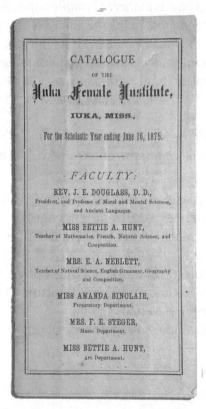

(Miss Lyla saved this impressive, well–prepared catalogue. See the APPENDIX – Chapter 29 Excerpt for details, including

Names of Pupils, Studies, Charges, General Remarks, Examination and Commencement Exercises and Board of Trustees.

For 1875, the course of Studies was quite impressive and extensive.)

Studies

PREPARATORY DEPARTMENT

Speller, Webster's
Readers, McGuffey's Series.
Geography, Mitchell's Series
Arithmetic, Written, Ray's Series.
                    Mental, Colburn's
English Grammar, Butler's and Hervey's

COLLEGIATE DEPARTMENT

ENGLISH BRANCHES

Quackenbos' Natural Philosophy.
Youman's Chemistry.
Woods' Object Lessons in Botany.
Coming's Physiology.
Olmsted's Astronomy.
Peterson's Familiar Science.
Barber's Geology.
Algebra, Davies'.
Geometry, Davies'.
Trigonometry –Plane, Analytical, Spherical, Davies'.
Quackenbos' Rhetoric
Elements of Mythology.
Steven's History of the United States.

Mitchell's large Geography.
Monteith's Physical Geography.
Smith's Etymology.
Quackenbos' Composition.
Hedges' Logic.
Rivers' Moral and Mental Philosophy.
Political Economy, Wayland.
Kames' Elements of Criticism.
Alexander's Evidence of Christianity.
Parsing – Pollock, Young, Milton.

LATIN

Spencer and Bullion's Grammar.
Reader.
Caesar.
Virgil.
Cicero.
Horace.
Arnold's Latin Prose Composition.

FRENCH

Fasquell's Course
Introductory.
Grammar.
Conversation.
Telemaque.
Corinne.
Racine.

(Under General Remarks there is a list of eight General Regulations. Number seven is especially interesting.)

GENERAL REGULATIONS

1. No student will be permitted to enter the Collegiate Department under twelve years of age, and then she must have a correct knowledge of the preparatory studies.
2. Students are admitted at any time, and charged from the week of entrance, inclusive. But those who delay their return, and permitted to advance with their classes, will be charged for the whole Session; and no deduction will be made for absence, except for sickness protracted one month, and then one-half of the charge will be returned or deducted.
3. No student will be admitted for less time than one Session, or the end of the current term.
4. Students are not permitted to take lessons of any kind out of the Institute on subjects taught in it, except by the special permission of the President.
5. Every student is required to be present at the opening and closing exercises, and deport herself with becoming respect and propriety.
6. Monthly reports will be sent to parents and guardians to advise them of the attendance, deportment, and scholarship of their daughters or wards.
7. Attending parties, or places of public amusement, and holding communication, written or verbal, during the Session, with gentlemen, except near relatives, are found to be prejudicial to success in study, and often result in evil consequences, and are therefore strictly forbidden. In fact, all letters will be subject to the inspection and revision of the Teachers, if necessary.
8. Boarding pupils are placed under the charge of the President, who provides for them in the regular boarding-house connected with the Institute; or, when it is thought best, obtains board in private families, and thus keeps them all subject to the same regulations.

CHAPTER 30

CATALOGUE OF THE IUKA FEMALE INSTITUTE AND IUKA MALE COLLEGE 1876-77

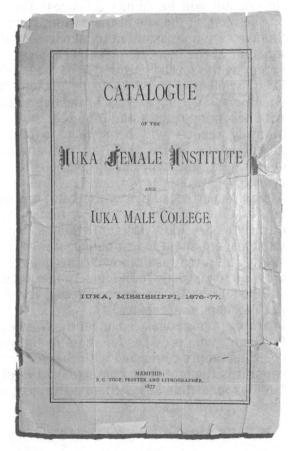

CATALOGUE

OF THE

IUKA FEMALE INSTITUTE

AND

IUKA MALE COLLEGE.

IUKA, MISSISSIPPI, 1876-77.

MEMPHIS:
S. C. TOOF, PRINTER AND LITHOGRAPHER.
1877

(This ten-page Catalogue of the Iuka Female Institute and Iuka Male College for the year 1876-77 gives the Board of Trustees, Faculty, Students, Course of Instruction, Sessions and Vacations, Terms per Session, Location and Calendar for both schools. Details in the APPENDIX – Chapter 30 Excerpt.)

*(**Food for thought:** There were 78 female and 56 male students enrolled in the 1876-77 session. Miss Lyla pointed out several times in her papers that during the Iuka Female Institute/Iuka Male College years under Flournoy and Pettus, the two schools were in different locations, across town from each other. With such a limited faculty and Flournoy and Pettus doing most of the teaching, it would be interesting to know how they did it).*

FACULTY (of the female institute)

N. A. Flournoy, A. M., President.
Ancient Languages and Literature, English Language and Literature, Mental and Moral Philosophy, and Book*keeping.

John C. Pettus, A. M., (U. Va.)
Modern Languages, Mathematics and Astronomy.

Miss M. Roselle Ferrill, M. A.,
Assistant in the Literary Departments, and Instructress of Calisthenics.

Miss Hattie E. Lealand, M. M.,
Music Department

FACULTY (of the male college)

John C. Pettus, A. M., (U. Va.) President
Ancient and Modern Languages, and Mathematics.

N. A. Flournoy, A. M.,
Book*keeping, Literature, Assistant in Ancient Languages [sic]

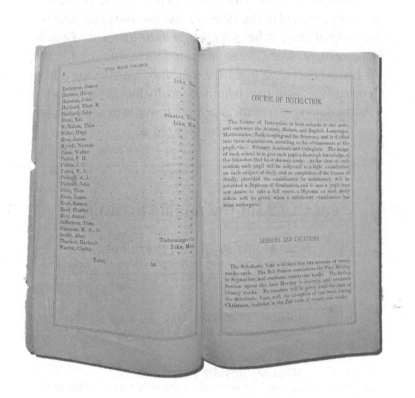

CHAPTER 31

THE "IUKA MIRROR" SUPPLEMENT
– M. A. SIMMONS, M.D.

*(Chapter 14 describes Dr. M. A. Simmons' almanac in 1856.
At that time, he was a resident of Jacinto, Mississippi. Later,
as a resident of Iuka, before moving to St. Louis, Missouri, he
had his own newspaper called the "Iuka Mirror."*

*Miss Lyla saved a now crumbling page printed front and
back from a paper called The "Iuka Mirror" Supplement,
which came after Dr. Simmons moved to St. Louis. The
"supplement" has no publication date but contains
references to the years 1879 and 1880. It also includes a
mineral analysis of the Iuka Springs (APPENDIX – Chapter
31 Excerpt) plus detailed descriptions of properties in Iuka
that Dr. Simmons wished to sell. The abbreviated versions of
Dr. Simmons' descriptions found here in Chapter 31 give an
interesting glance at downtown Iuka in the 1880s.*

*When reading Dr. Simmons' picturesque descriptions, be
patient with his 150-year-old writing. Imagine your way
through houses, past gardens and fences, down alleyways,
and across streets of long ago. It is worthy of note that
all the businesses along Fulton and Front streets in Iuka
burned in a massive fire in March 1896. Most likely, that
fire consumed several of the properties described here by
Dr. Simmons.)*

eing well and permanently settled in St. Louis, Mo., will sell property elsewhere at low prices.

Printing Office and Weekly Paper.

The "Iuka Mirror" office cost me at least twelve hundred dollars. The press is a Smith press. It is the heaviest and most steady hand press I ever saw. It makes as good impressions as a power press. The office is entire, full and complete. A paper and card cutter that cost me fifty dollars in New York, two excellent imposing stones, a nice little cabinet, copper roller-mold, plenty metal galleys, cases, stands, chases, rules, sticks, etc. I would take cash for the office and goodwill of the "Mirror" ($500) five hundred dollars.

Two Lucky, Convenient and Pleasant Store Houses Together.

The drug store house on the north side of the Public Square near the railway depot on the northeast corner of Main street and the Public Square is one of the best stands for any kind of business in the town. In this house is where the writer kept a drug store at least ten years and made most of the property he now owns. The house covers the whole lot, 25 by 90 feet.

At the fireplace on the north side of the chimney is a nice bedroom for sleeping, resting and private study. There is a window in the west and a stairway to the garret. This is cut off from the north end of the house by a solid plank partition. The door in this partition opens into a hall through the house from the street into the backyard, where there is a well of excellent water and a wood yard, both near the east door. At the north side of this hall are a glass partition and glass-door shutter opening into a large room which has a fireplace and a chimney at the north end and three windows. **This room is now, and has for many years been the "Iuka Mirror" printing office.**

The fence around the backyard is eight and a half feet high and has a gate with lock and key opening on a twenty-feet alley at the north end of these lots. On about twenty feet of the south end of this lot is one of the most popular store houses in the town. It is the full width of the lot, twenty-five feet, about fifteen feet deep and has a chimney and fireplace in the south end plus a large double door and two windows in the south side on the Public Square. I would take cash, ($1,500) fifteen hundred dollars for these two houses and lots.

Two Store Rooms and Private Boarding House.

A two-story store house near the center of the same block above-named, on the north side of the Public Square, is arranged for a private boarding house and restaurant in connection with the store. Here a poor man can get a start and make a good living without capital and with little labor if he only has something for his own family to eat. Others would gladly eat with them and pay twenty-five cents each. Twenty-five cents a meal is low in that country, yet it pays well. This house covers the full width of the lot - twenty-five feet.

The kitchen in the backyard is a good house, floored with brick, plenty of light and a brick flue for the stovepipe. There is also room for wood. The fence is eight-and-a-half feet high with a door, lock and key, in the north end for access to a twenty feet alley.
There are three rooms above the stairs in this house. For this lot and improvements, I would take cash ($700) seven hundred dollars.

The Nearest Residence Place to all Businesses and Churches.

On the opposite side of this twenty feet alley, above mentioned, at the north end of the store house lots, is the most conspicuous family residence place and the nearest to all the business houses and churches in town. It includes five lots. Upon the two east lots that lie across the block from the alley to Eastport Street is a beautiful and convenient cottage residence fronting Eastport Street. **This place is on the southeast corner of Main and Eastport streets, opposite the Methodist Church.** I would take cash ($800) eight hundred dollars for these five lots and improvements.

A Self-Supporting Home.

On the opposite side of Main street, from the place last above described between the same alley and Eastport street, on the southwest corner of Main and Eastport streets, is a self-supporting home for even a lazy man by an outlay of about two hundred and fifty or three hundred dollars for a little engine grist mill. It is also a good stand for a private boarding house and a store. It includes six lots, and all the block except two lots occupied by the Baptist Church on the northwest corner of the block. The dwelling house in the enclosure, near the southwest corner of Main and Eastport streets, is one-story, about thirty feet wide by eighty feet long, east and west.

The mill house and crib have large doors on the alley for receiving and sending out produce. The stable is west of the crib under the same roof. The engine house joins the mill house over the door at the past side under which is a well of pure water for the engine and for stock. The mill house and stack for the engine are near the depot and only one hundred and ten feet from the Public Square. For these six lots and improvements, I would take, now, cash, ($1,500) Fifteen hundred dollars.

A Lucky Home.

North of this place, across Eastport Street, on the northwest corner of Main and Eastport, opposite the Methodist Church, which is on the northeast corner of these streets, is one of the most convenient and pleasant little cottages in the town. There are three rooms, a stack chimney, plenty of sash-balanced windows and a portico and hall in the front corner house. It sits back from the corner leaving a little front yard. About eight or ten feet north of it is the kitchen. There is space between the houses covered and floored, making a nice room.

For these two lots and improvements, I would take, now, cash ($700) seven hundred dollars.

The Lowest Priced Home.

On the west end of the same block of the place last described, on a wide street that runs north and south- -its name is forgotten (*Pearl Street*)—**on the northeast corner of this street and Eastport Street, opposite the Baptist church, which is on the southeast corner of these streets, is a beautiful place,** less improvements, however, and therefore, less price. It includes two and a half lots, 62½×90 feet, enclosed upon cedar posts. The house has two rooms, a stack chimney, two fireplaces, plenty of windows, a well of excellent water and is the same distance from the Public square as the place last above described, in the same block. For these lots, I would take ($250), two hundred and fifty dollars.

The Best Drug Store.

My drug store in - Iuka was one of the fullest and most complete, convenient and best arranged that anybody ever saw anywhere. For the whole of which I would take now cash ($800) eight hundred dollars.

Medicines.

I have sold my liver medicine business, in which you encouraged me so liberally for nearly forty years, and rented the laboratory and residence with it to the party. Have recently bought No. 2733 Clark Avenue (St. Louis) for another laboratory to manufacture my Purifying Pills, the best natural tonic; my compound Essence of Assofoetida, the best natural anodyne; my Cholera Syrup, Cough Syrup, Alterative, Acoustic Drops, Tooth-ache Cure and others which thousands of you know, from having used them, to be reliable and sure to accomplish all that is claimed for them. All liberal physicians acknowledge my views of theory and practice and recommend my preparations. I hope to send you notices soon that I am ready to fill orders. I write thus familiarly to all the inhabitants of the world, without exception, because all have proved to be long tried, faithful friends to me. I will be thankful for letters from any of you upon any subject.

Dear old correspondents, please write, that I may know you still live.

I am your old friend,

M. A. SIMMONS, M.D.
2733 Clark Avenue,
St. Louis, Mo.

CHAPTER 32

BROCHURE FOR THE IUKA
NORMAL INSTITUTE IN 1883

(Impressive 12-page, foldout brochure for the Iuka Normal Institute in 1883. It is quite detailed, with numerous topics discussed (Faculty, Calendar, Location, Terms and Expenses, Normal School, Normal Method of Teaching Rhetoric, General Literature, Natural Sciences, Training Department and Course of Study). The two topics enclosed here, "Normal School" and "Course of Study," give insight into the philosophy, teaching methods and scope of the INI – included word for word. The remaining topics are in the APPENDIX – Chapter 32 Excerpt.

Even though the Institute existed for only about twenty years (1882 –1901), its praises were still sung well into the mid-twentieth century and beyond. Autrey Mangum, in his history of Iuka, Down Memory Lane, published in 1971, said, "Except for the mineral waters, and as a health resort, Iuka has never been better and more favorably known than by the Iuka Normal Institute.")

111

NORMAL SCHOOL.

—o—

What is a Normal School? The popular idea is, that it
is suitable only for teachers, for those who expect to

follow teaching as a business. This is very erroneous. The primary meaning of the word, Normal, is a straight line, the shortest distance between two points. Hence, technically, it is the shortest and most practicable route (line) from the point ignorance, to the point, intelligence; from impotency of will, the "I can't" of pupils to the active will force, the "I can try," the I WILL, which has, from earth's poverty stricken ones, made giants in spite of the want of a book education.

Normal means natural. Hence, strictly, Normal methods are in accord with mind and human experience out of the School room, methods which put the student to evolving will power, the ability to do something with mind, muscle and heart, methods which enable the student to get control of all his powers and to use them for whatever his hand and the world may find for him to do.

Common sense, the requisite to success in actual life, is found everywhere except in the school room with the children. The methods of instruction of the dark ages are still found in the district school and in the university. What is common sense in the school room? How are men and women trained in actual life? The world, or necessity, puts them to trying to make a living. Our best businessmen served a long apprenticeship, before they could manipulate a trade palace. Our greatest statesmen had a struggle for existence before they were immortalized by a nation's vote and homage. Our successful farmers are men, seven times out of ten, who studied farming while a boy following a mule in the hot sun. Perhaps one minister in a hundred has a college diploma. A young man feels himself called to preach, the church puts him to exhorting, singing, praying, preaching and in a few years he is a polished, forcible speaker, a holy man. Actual work gives him power to work.

Now, apply this worldly wisdom to the school room. Do you wish your boy to be a linguist? Put him to reading the languages, not to committing grammars. Do you want him to understand surveying? Give him the instruments and books and put him to measuring land. Do you wish your daughter to be able to write a decent letter? Put her to writing letters, not to pouring over some "fraud'" letter writer. Do you want your boy to be a speaker? Give him subjects and references to books and put him to making speeches.

The above is the Normal method for the whole curriculum. This gives power, the legitimate aim of all school work. Huxley says: "The most valuable result of all education, is the ability to make yourself to do the thing you have to do when it ought to be done, whether you like to do it or not." Knowledge is not power, but the ability to do a thing and then the doing of it is power.

Normal schools are a necessity. There are 300,000 teachers in the United States; 250,000 in the district schools. Four years is the average time to each teacher in the profession. The teacher thus leaves the school room just as his experience begins to make him efficient. Consequently, the children are not half taught. But is the Normal trained teacher any better? W. T. Harris, the distinguished educator and superintendent, says; "The teacher trained in a Normal school is the equal of the teacher who has had ten years actual experience in the school room." Education is a science and should be studied and applied in the school room by the teacher. Many think Normal schools are only for training teachers. The farmer, the lawyer, the mechanic, the minister, the female world must go somewhere else. Since Normals only teach how to teach, only the profession should attend them. Now let us examine this idea. The intelligent will admit them to be a necessity for the teacher. The same studies are taught in all first-class Normals that are taught in colleges and seminaries. Further, if they are a necessity for the teacher, they are, for those to be taught. If the education needed for success in life cannot be had in a Normal school, then the teacher ought not to attend them. If he does not get in the Normal what the world wants, then he is not fit to teach the youths of the country; for these are to be trained by the teacher for the practical actualities of life. Education must be social, mental and moral. This education by means of books and nature is the grand aim of the Normal school; but this is the demand of the age. This demand is the cause for the existence of the Normal school. Hence, it is a valuable school for any one to attend who desire a practical education.

COURSE OF STUDY.

-:0:-

1. PREPARATORY.

5th Reader, Spelling and Letter Writing, Geography Completed, Arithmetic Completed, Grammar and Analysis, Hygiene, Elementary Algebra, Composition, Specimens in Literature, Elocution and Drawing, Debate.

2. TEACHERS' OR SCIENTIFIC JUNIOR, ONE YEAR.

1. Studies-Arithmetic, Algebra and Geometry Completed, Map Drawing, Physiology, Natural Philosophy, Pedagogies, Rhetoric, Grammar, Beginning Latin or German.

115

2. Drills--Methods and Management, Letter Writing, U. S. History and Constitution, Debating and Parliamentary Law, Drawing, Elocution and Penmanship.

3. SCIENTIFIC SENIOR OR CLASSICS JUNIOR, ONE YEAR.

1. Studies-Trigonometry, Analytic Geometry, Calculus, Dif. and Integ., Math. Astronomy; Botany, Zoology, Chemistry, Geology ; Cæsar, Cicero, Virgil, German, Mental Science.

2. Drills-History of England, France, Rome and Greece; American Poets, English Poets, Shakespeare, Milton and Debating; Elocution, Music and Rhetoric.

4. CLASSIC SENIOR, ONE YEAR.

1. Studies--Logic with Argument, Criticism with Essays, Ethics and Law, Social Science; Horace, Livy and Tacitus; Begin Greek, New Testament, Xenophon, Homer.

2. Drills--Lectures by pupils, on Philosophy, Profane History, Sacred History ; Debating, Orations, Outlines on Roman History, Grecian History, Jewish History and Philology and Ethnology.

Economical Print, 122 Union St., Nashville, Tenn.

CHAPTER 33

IUKA NORMAL INSTITUTE BOOKLET 1883-84 LIST OF STUDENTS AND GRADUATES

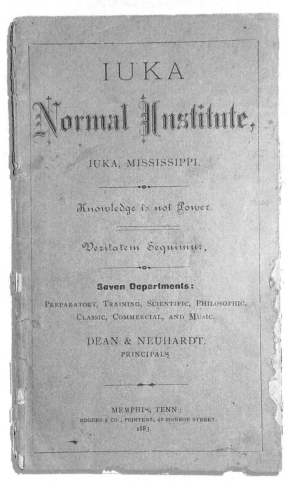

IUKA

Normal Institute,

IUKA, MISSISSIPPI.

Knowledge is not Power.

Veritatem Sequimur.

Seven Departments:

PREPARATORY, TRAINING, SCIENTIFIC, PHILOSOPHIC, CLASSIC, COMMERCIAL, AND MUSIC.

DEAN & NEUHARDT,
PRINCIPALS

MEMPHIS, TENN.:
ROGERS & CO., PRINTERS, 42 MONROE STREET.
1883.

(This 24-page booklet goes to great lengths in explaining the Normal teaching method and, for the most part, duplicates the information and descriptions found in the foldout brochure discussed in Chapter 32.

The Iuka Normal Institute was established in 1882 by H. A. Dean & John Neuhardt. The brochure here, in Chapter 33, lists ten graduates for 1883, most likely the first graduates of the INI. The list of 148 undergraduates set to begin the new term on September 3, 1883, is in the APPENDIX – Chapter 33 Excerpt.)

Graduates of 1883

W. A. Belk	– Clay Co., Miss.	D. B. President
Mattie Deardolph	– Tishomingo Co. Miss.	D. B. Cor. Secy.
A. H. Flynt	– "	D. B. Orator
Arthur Harvey	– "	D. B. Historian
Bessie Johnson	– "	D. B. Vice Pres.
C. Kendrick	– "	A. B.
F. M. Malone	– DeSoto Co., Miss.	D. B. Poet
Lula Petty	– Lee County, Miss.	D. B. Secy
J. I. Robinson	– Tishomingo Co. Miss.	D. B
J. F. Yow	– "	D. B. Prophet

118

CHAPTER 34

NEWSPAPER FOR THE IUKA NORMAL INSTITUTE 1885 (NUMBER I, VOLUME I)

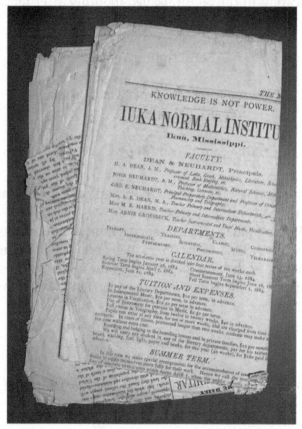

(Found in Miss Lyla's papers, these five extremely ragged newspaper pages [3 through 8] are most likely from the first

issue of the INSTITUTE, published by Dean and Neuhardt of the Iuka Normal Institute. On the top left-hand corner of page 4, it says:)

The Normal Institute
published by
Dean & Neuhardt.

An educational journal, devoted to the cause of education in the South, issued monthly after January, 1885.

Subscription Terms:

By mail, payable in advance, postage
prepaid, per annum.........$1.00
Six months........................... 50
One month, one copy........... 10

No. I. Volume I. – Twenty thousand copies are sent out free as sample copies.

No. II., Volume I., will be issued, twenty thousand copies, in July, 1884. Subscribers may order the July number alone, or they can begin their year's subscription and thus get thirteen numbers of the INSTITUTE for one dollar.

Iuka, Miss. January 28, 1884

(Also on Page 4 there is this paragraph under Notice to Advertisers:)

The Iuka Normal Institute, Iuka, Miss., is now in its second half year, and has enrolled over 300 students.

The graduates and teachers sent out by this institution are wide awake, up with the times and having wonderful success. Persons desiring a practical common-sense and thorough education, in the shortest time possible and with the least expense, can do no better than to attend this school.

(Among several topics on Page 4 is
Golden Rules for Boys and Girls:)

1. Shut the door after you, and without slamming it.
2. Never shout, jump or run in the house.
3. Never call to persons upstairs or in the next room; if you wish to speak to them go quietly where they are.
4. Always speak quietly and kindly to the servants, if you would have them do the same to you.
5. When told to do or not to do a thing, by either parent, never ask why you should or should not do it.
6. Tell of your own faults and misdoings, not those of your brothers and sisters.
7. Carefully clean the mud or snow off your boots before entering the house.
8. Be prompt at every meal hour.
9. Never sit down at the table, or in the parlor, with dirty hands or tumbled hair.
10. Never interrupt any conversation.

(Most of the information found on pages 5 through 8 is
devoted to the text of a lecture entitled THE SOUTH; OR A
VERY INTERESTING INVALIDE given by H. A. Dean in the
spring of 1881 to the students and faculty of the National
Normal Institute, Lebanon, Ohio. According to the article,
even though sixteen years had passed since the close of the
War Between the States, the South was still struggling

to find its footing. Mr. Dean provides a solution. The first and last paragraphs of his lengthy article are included.)

Friends, we have met as attendant and consulting physicians. The patient lies wholly south of Mason and Dixon's line, but not at the point of death; she is not complaining much. Frequently, she very earnestly contends that she is not even sick; but some of her own family and all her neighbors believe there is some terrible disease preying on her vitals. Her family and friends have nursed her very closely since '65. Then the patient was sick almost unto death, but she has been gradually gaining strength and otherwise improving up to the present time.

(After three newspaper pages, Mr. Dean ends his article with...)

The diagnosis and prescription are submitted to you for your thoughtful consideration.

H. A. DEAN

(Advertisers in this first issue of the INSTITUTE stretch from Iuka to New York City.)

little stiff-necked, or
slow in trying costly
of destitution. Thi
doubtless próved ve
Hindoostan, or som
islands of old ocea
was not quite the pr
case. It was a little
siasm of our North
She "sat up into the
night," knitting wool
shirts and petti oats
South, when the neg
would have been mo
brella and linen duste
siasm was all right, b
wrong channel. S
doctor. His king-c
it had been a heathe
patient is not a heath
to the case. These p
in their diagnoses, of
were worse than usel
The family physi
time presented his
and presents the m a
this consultation.
and true conclusio n
we must, if possibl on
of the disease. Wil
a prescription will be
The first symptom
itself soon after the
something over two
slight pimple was se
tient's cheek. This
1620, at Jamestown,
this was at that time
chief elements of th

124

t the one who
ildren." This
utside of the
erywhere else
eplies, but is
the rule. It
y with eight
hardly large
est.' Friends:

mind us,
ll;
as
,"

the capital,
igration, the
e well mixed
f the element

d greatly in
hools. This
out the first
these two,
the present
free schools
ildren cause
l-houses and
the demand
ry expenses,
red a limited
st 'persevere
mon-school
every child,

ited in in-
free schools
/ beneficial,
nded as to
they employ
nds to pay
as to place
State and
al, success-
,hands of
nisters and

be overcome
outh. The
t by cheap
t but

would be true sentinels guarding the battle-field of Ideas.

The essence of the prescription is to the patient is most important part. Without Christianity the other elements would prove a curse. I had rather there would never be another school-house built in the South than to have a godless system of schools. The heathen is a law unto himself; but an intellectual skepticism has a revealed law to obey or suffer its penalties. Unlettered faith is surely preferable to scientific Huxleyism. The Christian graces—faith, hope and charity—are many times more valuable to the patient than classic Bob Ingersollism.

The diagnosis and prescription are submitted to you for your thoughtful consideration.

H. A. DEAN.

CHAPTER 35

HISTORICAL REMINISCENCES OF EAST TENNESSEE – JOHN NEUHARDT
(Included as Chapter 35 for one reason and one reason alone are the FIRST AND LAST PARAGRAPHS of a seven-page essay on lined paper held together by a straight pin – it is well-written and beautifully scripted by one of the founders of the Iuka Normal Institute, John Neuhardt.)

(First Paragraph)

In this age of American energy for the accumulation of wealth, and in the struggle, on the other hand, to discourage this energy by abnormal legislation, it is a pleasant relief to recall the early struggles and events of those who settled, colonized, and shaped the destiny of our country. I have selected a few incidents only from the early history of East Tennessee. These incidents are from data collected during a sojourn in Jefferson County.

(Last Paragraph)

In the city of Knoxville, I had the pleasure of visiting the Sevier Mansion. Introducing myself to the owner, Dr. Park, I added that I have the good fortune of possessing a wife who is a great-great-granddaughter of Governor John Sevier, who laid the foundation of this mansion and built its brick walls to the first floor. The brick and mortar in this mansion are perfectly sound. The panel-work inside, the mantelpiece, and woodwork are all beautiful designs - handsome, and hand-carved, without a crack or misfit. This historic mansion is fully worth one's visit and observation.

(John Neuhardt's wife was Miss Lyla's sister, Effie Merrill. Effie and Miss Lyla were both great-great-granddaughters of John Sevier, the first governor of Tennessee.)

127

CHAPTER 36

TINTYPE PHOTOGRAPH OF MISS LYLA'S SISTER – EFFIE MERRILL TAKEN IN 1867 AT AGE 5 YEARS

(On the back, Miss Lyla has written "Sister Effie Aged 5 Yrs 1867.)

EFFIE MERRILL

CHAPTER 37

BAPTISMAL CERTIFICATE OF
EDWIN NEUHARDT

(This beautiful baptismal certificate found folded in Miss Lyla's papers is written in German and says that Edwin Neuhardt was born in Iuka, Mississippi, on December 28, 1884, to John Neuhardt and Effie Merrill Neuhardt. Edwin's baptism was on August 7, 1887. Where in Iuka the baptism took place is not mentioned. There are three Bible verses written on the certificate in German – one in the oval near the center top and the other two in scrolls on the left side and bottom.)

Matthew 28:19 – Therefore go and teach all nations and baptize them in the name of the Father and of the Son and of the Holy Spirit.

Mark 16:16 – Who believes and is baptized will, he will be saved.

Mark 10:14 – Let the little children come to me, for such is the Kingdom of God.

CHAPTER 38

PRIVATE JOHN ALLEN

(Miss Lyla typed a 15-page life story of John Mills Allen and fastened it together with a rusty needle. Several pages are splattered with ink as though a bottle tipped over during writing. Selected paragraphs from this essay connect nicely to paint a short, colorful picture of the man known as Private John Allen.)

Iuka, Mississippi July 25

The recently revived interest in the life of that odd, lovable character, Private John M. Allen, who in years past brought worthy notice to Mississippi and whose rare sense of humor healed many a sore spot in the awful years following the Civil War, that rare son of the Old South "who fit, bled and died" for the land he loved so well but who put away rancor after its doom was sealed at Appomattox, makes one glad to know that he was a product of old Tishomingo County.

His first race for Congress was in 1880 against General W. S. Tucker and Colonel S. M. Meek. In this memorable campaign, he won the name of Private John Allen, the only private he said who came out of the (Civil) war. The occasion was related by citizens now living in Iuka who attended the speaking in Corinth:

131

General Tucker said to the voters, "Seventeen years ago, my fellow citizens, after a hard-fought battle on yonder hill, I bivouacked under yonder clump of trees. Those who remember as I do the times that tried men's souls will not forget your humble servant when the primary shall be held."

Thereupon John Allen arose and said, "My fellow citizens, what General Tucker said about having bivouacked in yonder clump of trees on yonder hill in that engagement seventeen years ago is true. It is also true, my fellow citizens, that I was vidette picket and stood guard over him while he slept. Now all of you who were generals and had privates stand guard over you while you slept, vote for General Tucker, and all of you who were privates and stood guard over generals while they slept vote, for Private John Allen."

None of the three received sufficient votes for election, and John Allen withdrew on the 368th ballot when Colonel Muldrow of Oktibbeha County was nominated.

In 1884 he was elected to Congress and served his district most acceptably for sixteen years. During his many terms as a congressman, his reputation as a humorist grew, a reputation that students of politics say is fatal to a man's political advancement. It brought John Allen the love and admiration of a nation and filled his soul, no doubt, with more joy and peace and less malice and jealousy than any high office could ever have done. His tongue was sharp, but there was no venom in it. And those who had occasion to feel it most were, in the end, his best friends. He entered Congress just when political history was in the bitterest stage and the Bloody Shirt was forever being dangled before the suffering South. It is said that he did more to heal the breach by his broad common sense and wit than any other man.

In this connection, another story is told by Judge Phillips, Commander of the Grand Army of the Republic. At a convention of that organization at Oconomowoc, Wisconsin, Colonel George Peck was toastmaster. Judge Phillips tells the story as follows:

Colonel Peck introduced me as the representative of the Union Army, to which I responded briefly. He then said that the occasion was rendered particularly happy in that there was present the only private in the Confederate army with the Star Spangled Banner floating over him, representing the best government on earth which John Allen had tried to destroy and now had for an audience the veterans of the army. Allen, cigar in mouth, rose and said, "Veterans of the Union Army, I never saw your faces before, but I saw your backs often during the war. But because a Southern soldier would not shoot a man in the back, you would all be in your graves tonight. You would not think in looking at the rotund, obese form of George Peck that he was a sprinter, yet for the fact that he could outrun a minie bullet, I would have shot him dead in battle. I am glad that I missed overtaking him; otherwise, we would not be here eating the rich things that came from the land which grows brave men and pumpkins."

Once in the halls of Congress, making a speech about the war, someone questioned a remark of his as to truthfulness. "And I fought against the Yankees, and in one bloody engagement, they captured me. After they had held me prisoner for a week, they turned me loose. I rejoined my regiment and took up the pleasant pastime of killing Yankees. They captured me again and, after another week, turned me loose once more."

But why, came an interruption from the floor, did they turn you loose instead of keeping you prisoner?

"Because they figured they'd rather fight me than feed me," he said.

His first speech in Congress, which brought him fame, was the one in 1886 against burying dead congressmen at the expense of the nation. Among other things, he said, "Sir, a dead congressman has become an expensive luxury to the American people. If we die paupers, it is our fault. We get a salary of $5,000 a year with four times as much mileage as it actually costs us and five times as much stationary as we use. Any member here could save enough from his mileage and stationery account to give him a decent burial."

Perhaps his greatest bid for fame was when he made the celebrated fish hatchery story in Congress, asking for a hatchery to be established in his hometown. He said, "Many of my colleagues have never been to Tupelo. I hope none of you entertain any idea of dying without going there. Come and see once of our silver moons. I think it is the only place in the world where we have the same moons we had before the war. While there are other places larger than Tupelo, I do not think there are any places just like it. Tupelo is very near the center of the world, if not exactly the center. The sun seems about the same distance in every direction. We have the ideal place for a fish factory. Why, sir, fish will travel overland for miles to get into the water we have at Tupelo. Thousands and millions of unborn fish are clamoring to

Congress today for an opportunity to be hatched at the Tupelo hatchery."

In the stirring days of 1898, when the United States was getting ready to take a hand in Cuban affairs and the jingoes at Washington were blaming President McKinley for not rushing in, General Grosvenor of Ohio called upon his colleagues to form a regiment under him. Allen drawled, "Mr. Speaker, I am a loyal American who would be delighted to serve under the leadership of the gentleman from Ohio, but there is a bar. I served four years as a private in the Confederate Army. A lot of my boys went out with me. With those who came back, it would be all right. There are a lot of the boys who wore the gray who did not come back, who have crossed the river and are resting under the shade of the trees. They don't know that the war is over and that General Grovesnor's folks licked the tar out of ours. If I went out with him wearing a blue uniform and got killed and went to heaven in that rig, those old fellows would look at me with surprise and say: John Allen deserted, damn him."

At the time of his death, which took place at his home in Tupelo on October 31, 1917, he was 72 years old. General Grosvenor, who made the bitter speech in Congress when he wanted to get the congressmen to form a regiment under him, died the same day. At Allen's death, newspapers all over the country carried tributes to him, coming from friend and political foes alike, all of whom paid homage to his rugged honesty and high principles.

CHAPTER 39

IUKA NORMAL INSTITUTE 1898
COMMENCEMENT EXERCISES

(Formal, well-done invitation to the INI Commencement Exercises of May 30 through June 4, 1898. For complete, typed details of each day's activities, see APPENDIX – Chapter 39 Excerpt.)

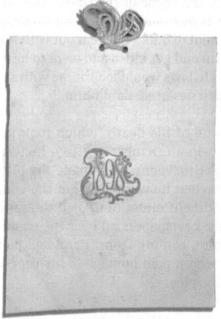

(After the Wednesday night banquet, the events of Thursday must have been a highlight for the town and not to be missed.)

Thursday Evening, June 2.

Artistic Presentations and Interpretations by Advanced
Music and Elocution Classes

1. Reading, "Aux Italieus," -   Owen Meredith
                Mrs. R. L. Shook.

2. Onomatopoetic, Tennyson's "Bugle Song,"   Class

3. Humorous Drama, "Place aux Dames."

                DRAMATIC PERSONAE.
                "Ophelia," Mattie Watson.
                "Portia," Birdie Dugger
                "Juliet," Zola McIntire
                "Lady Macbeth," Mrs. McIntire

4. Greek Romance, from the German by Frederick
   Helm.
                "Parthenai," Miss Victoria McCay.
                "Ingomar," J. E. Blythe.

5. Reading, "Minister's Housekeeper," – H. B. Stowe

6. Shaftsbury Tableaux Plastique, – Class

                Louise E. Anthony, Directress of Music
                L. Pierce H. McIntire, Directress of Expression

CHAPTER 40

MARCH 27 – THAT FATEFUL DAY

(Miss Lyla typed two versions of this story and sewed all the pages together at the top with needle and thread. Of the two versions, the first is the most detailed and complete.)

Iuka, Mississippi March 27.

March 27th has been, through the years, an eventful day for Iuka and Tishomingo County.

On March 27, 1857, workers completed the Memphis and Charleston Railroad in Iuka, and a grand celebration took place. Crews working on the construction came from east and west, and the lines came together about five hundred feet from where the railroad station now stands. A golden spike was to mark the completion. High officials from the various roads that constituted the Memphis and Charleston, plus governors and other dignitaries, were to make speeches at the ceremony. There was a barbecue with wines and other liquors, and all went merry until the distinguished gentleman, who was to drive the spike, took charge. So long and so well had he provided for the inner man that he could no longer hold the mallet nor hit the spike. Time and time again, he tried. Time and time again, he failed amid first the titering which gave way to uproarious laughter. Seeing at last that he could not perform the task assigned him and complaining of a sudden spell of vertigo, he turned to a common laborer standing by with a pick and shovel and said, "Pat can you drive a spike?"

"Faith and Begorry, sir, I'd be ashamed if I couldn't," said Pat. With one mighty lunge, the spike was in place.

Iuka remembers March 27, 1900, with sadness. That was the day when Mississippi's beloved ex-governor and Iuka's most illustrious citizen, John Marshall Stone, was brought back to be buried among the hills he loved so well. Governor Stone, always called Colonel Stone here, died in Holly Springs while serving his first term as president of A. and M. College at Starkville. Special trains ran on both Mobile and Ohio and Southern Railroads to bring the crowds of sorrowing citizens and students from the college to attend the funeral. Bishop Charles B. Galloway preached the funeral sermon, a matchless oration remembered to this day. Cadets from the college sounded taps over all that was mortal of the peerless John M. Stone, soldier, statesman and college president. His grave in Oak Grove Cemetery is marked with a towering shaft on which is engraved:

Twelve years Governor of Mississippi, Colonel of the Second Mississippi Regiment, Davis Brigade, President A. and M. College, Past Grand Master of Mississippi Masons, Eminent Commander Knights of Phythias.

Then on March 27, 1950, a disastrous cyclone visited the county and all but erased from the map the little town of Paden, Mississippi, about 15 miles southwest of Iuka. It destroyed churches, demolished the Masonic Hall, and blew away homes. Nearly every house in the little town suffered in some way.

CHAPTER 41

TURN OF THE CENTURY

(Three paragraphs from an incomplete, handwritten document with pages numbered 7 through 13 give insight into Iuka's transition from the 19th to the 20th century.)

The turn of the century brought many changes. In 1901 Iuka had its first electric lights, which was certainly an improvement over the old coal oil lamps. Even then the oil lamps had to be filled and trimmed, ready to be called into service during a church meeting or graduation exercises when the nearest neighbors had to scurry home and bring back the lighting. In 1914 the plant burned. From then until 1925, primitive lighting was all we had until the Mississippi Power Company came in with great blowing of trumpets. As with the railroad's completion in 1857, a big celebration took place at the Spring Park. The governor of the state, the president of the Mississippi Power Company with high officials, the president of the Alabama Power Company and representatives, the State president of the Mississippi Federation of Women's Clubs and many other celebrities had parts on the program. Mississippi Power Company furnished the barbecue for about 8,000 people who came from far and near. At that time, the Mississippi Power Company planned to build a dam on Bear Creek to furnish electric power for North Mississippi, an idea abandoned following the creation of TVA.

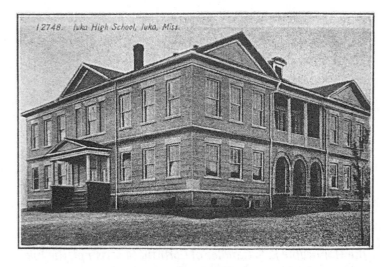

IUKA HIGH SCHOOL

In 1908 the town built the first of its brick school buildings, and for a time during construction, school convened in the courthouse. The old building which had been the first female institute, the hospital and morgue after the battle of Iuka, and the first Iuka Normal Institute building, was demolished to prepare the school site.

In 1908 the Illinois Central Railroad built a Birmingham branch through the county. Iuka had been the receiving and distribution point for the entire county and nearby counties and states, with freight brought as far as 60 miles by wagon. Now Tishomingo, Paden, Holcut, Dennis, Belmont and Golden joined the ranks of railroad towns in the county.

141

CHAPTER 42

IUKA NORMAL INSTITUTE 1901
INVITATION TO GRADUATION

*(This six-day event took place from Sunday, June 2nd
through Friday, June 7th with Mrs. T. M. McDonald giving
the Alumni Essay on Tuesday, June 4th. For the details of
each day's activities, see APPENDIX − Chapter 42 Excerpt.*

*After the Baccalaureate Address on Friday night by
the Honorable E. S. Candler of Corinth, Mississippi, the Iuka
Normal Institute conferred degrees to its last class. In a
matter of months, the INI closed its door forever.)*

CHAPTER 43

"WHERE SHALL I SPEND MY VACATION?"

(Miss Lyla kept four brochures [three different] entitled "Where Shall I Spend My Vacation?" All are similar in design, information, format and photographs. There are no publication dates, but contents indicate printing after the World's Fair in 1904.)

Where Shall I Spend My Vacation?

The eternal question – the one that comes to the tired businessman and weary housewife; the question which confronts the young man, pleasure bent; the one which comes to the sweet girl graduate; yes, the one which presents itself to the sufferer of disease – all must find a place, free from the cares and worries of their daily life; all must find a place where Nature, in her bountiful providence, has caused the sparkling waters to flow, the trees to grow luxuriant with shade, the place where the hum-drum of today may be buried beneath the spirit of "care-free rest," a desire for which inhabits every human heart.

Such a place is Iuka, Mississippi. Nature has never designed a place so beautiful in natural fitness, and endowed it with such wonderful waters.

Seven springs, now beautifully enclosed within a nature park of some eight or ten acres, peacefully flow, and any who will may come, without money and without price and partake of their wonderful power.

PARK SCENE

Many are the springs which Nature, in her goodness, has sprinkled over the face of the country; yet none of them have, by actual test, the wonderful purity and real medical power that is found in Iuka. At the World's Fair at St. Louis, one hundred and sixty different kinds of mineral waters were placed in competition. The experts of the world examined them all. Each was tested with every known test. Iuka's Mineral Water was awarded the Silver Medal; and that, too, in competition with The World.

IUKA MINERAL WATER

The Accommodations of Iuka

This question is the uppermost one in the mind of the average reader: Where shall I stay? What shall I find? No place can answer better than Iuka.

MINERAL SPRINGS HOTEL

The past year has been a busy one for the people of Iuka. The Mineral Springs Hotel, a very commodious brick building, has been rearranged; every room thoroughly overhauled and tastefully decorated. New furniture has been installed, private baths -- hot and cold water – modern public toilets and baths, intercommunicating telephones, and every convenience have been installed. The pictures herein contained express far better than words the transformation which has taken place in the hotel.

The Annex building and the cottages have been put in the best of order, refurnished and refitted throughout; and today, the Iuka Mineral Springs Hotel is as modern as modern fittings can make it.

PHOTOS FROM THE INTERIOR OF MINERAL SPRINGS HOTEL

The Leatherwood, another modern hotel of Iuka, has also been put in the best of condition. This popular place has been overhauled, hot and cold water, private and public baths, new paper and furniture and other modern conveniences have been installed. It affords the very best, and it is well located, upon a prominence, with every room an outside one, thoroughly lighted with electric lights, and is a credit to the now excellent hotel facilities of Iuka. This hotel is under the personal supervision of W. B. Leatherwood and wife, which guarantees the most exacting attention to its guests.

LEATHERWOOD HOTEL

The various boarding houses and hotels of Iuka have completely met the question of cuisine. A competent superintendent in charge of the Iuka Mineral Springs Hotel supplies the best from the markets of the larger cities every day. As mentioned above, W. B. Leatherwood and wife personally direct the Leatherwood Hotel and have always maintained a record for excellence of their table.

Perchance the reader may, for various reasons, wish to find a resting place less expensive than the hotels, though the rates quoted by them bring unexcelled service within the reach of all. However, there are those who prefer, for various reasons, various accommodations. Iuka has the very best of every grade. Within these pages will be found a list of hotels and boarding houses which accommodate the demands of every person. They are each and every one delightful places, and they serve the fat of the land to their guests. Their accommodations are good, and the wonderful waters of Iuka's Mineral Springs are ABSOLUTELY FREE TO ALL.

"THE CEDARS"

The Cedars – The beautiful colonial home of Mrs. E. N. Reed is literally enveloped in the evergreen and historic cedars. This home is most inviting and appeals to all summer visitors.

"BREEZY HILL"

Breezy Hill – Mrs. (Hattie) Doan's spacious home is situated on a beautiful hill, not more than a hundred yards from the Park. This is an ideal resting place where ever and anon the gentle breezes calm and soothe the tired or health-seeking visitor.

MINERAL SPRINGS BOARDING HOUSE

A. D. Langston, proprietor, is situated only around the corner from the Park. A comfortable and convenient place for the recruiting visitor. Splendid fare.

MRS. ELLEN LUKER

Mrs. Ellen Luker conducts a most pleasant and desirable boarding house only two blocks from Spring Park. Centrally located, convenient to the station, post office and churches.

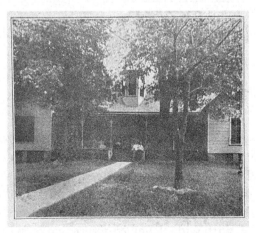

"OAK ARMS"

151

Mrs. C. W. McKnight's spacious and ideal Southern home is nestled in the arms of immense water oaks and is situated only across the street from the Park. This is a most desirable place for rest and recreation.

COTTAGE HOTEL, MRS. McKNIGHT, SAM ALLEN, MRS. R. T. RUTLEDGE

The Park Amusements and Pleasures

The scenes herein shown give a slight conception of the beauty of Iuka's beautiful park. This enclosure of some eight or ten acres, perfectly shaded by forest trees, is the property of the city of Iuka, and it is for the free use of all who will come. It has been traversed, from end to end, with wide, level, concrete walks, while under the spreading branches have been erected a Dancing

Pavilion, Bowling Alleys, Tennis Courts, Moving Picture show and a multiplicity of seats. The Park will be, this season, a paradise for the tired and weary. It will afford recreation, pleasure and change for every person. It is beautifully lighted with electric lights at night, and is an ideal spot to spend many a delightful hour sipping the waters and enjoying the company of friends and chance acquaintances.

A talented band will supply the necessary music for the lovers of dancing and music. Tennis and such favorite amusements are to be had, and not a single moment need hang upon the hands of the visitor.

Bathing at Iuka Lake, Iuka, Miss.

LAKE COMO

Lake Como and surroundings are the most beautiful and picturesque in our Southland. Nowhere does nature so appeal to the human heart as this lovely place.

Beautiful Lake Como Park is situated only one-half mile from Iuka depot consisting of 160 acres, of which 25 acres is the lake, well stocked with Black Bass, Trout, White Perch, Blue Cat and Bream. It has eight beautiful steel-lined row boats, a swimming pool, 20 room bath house, and an abundant supply of bathing suits for gentlemen, ladies and children.

The ideal pleasure resort and picnic grounds for Iuka visitors. Swings, lawn tennis, beautiful shade, spring water, etc. Resident family on the grounds.

Hack and Auto service to and from the lake daily, 25¢ round trip. Open from 5 a. m. to 10 p. m.

CHAPTER 44

PHOTOGRAPHS FROM A "SCRAPBOOK"

*(Fascinating, 4-page "scrapbook" type folder with photos
and newspaper clippings glued to the pages. The folder itself
is an amazing item. It is a large, four-page receipt from
an unknown source that is handwritten in brown ink with
a quill pen. The edges, especially the top and bottom, are
fragile, crumbling and missing some pieces. The writing
is very fancy. At the top of the first page are the words
Tuscumbia January 23, 184 [the last number looks to be a 5].
Described here in Chapter 44 are two photos – one from the
first page and one from the last.)*

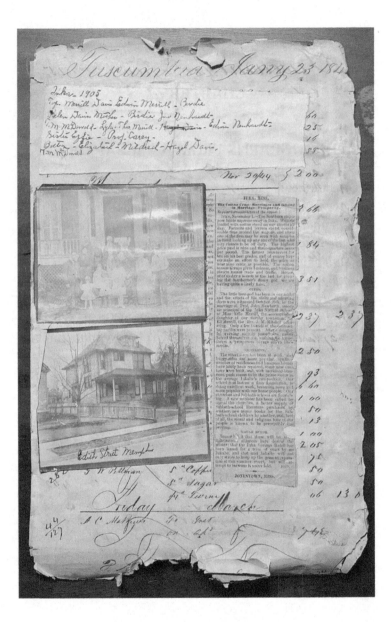

FIRST PAGE OF THE "SCRAPBOOK"

MERRILL/MCDONALD FAMILY PHOTO WITH LIST OF NAMES
(Possibly in front of the McDonald Home)

Iuka – 1905

Top. Merrill Davis – Edwin Merrill – Birdie
Helen Davis – Mother – Birdie – John Neuhardt
T. M. McDonald – Lyla – Thomas Merrill – Edwin Neuhardt
Sister Effie – Professor Carey
Bottom – Elizabeth –Mildred – Hazel Davis
T. M. McDonald

DUN ROBIN
Iuka, Mississippi

(Judging from the automobile parked in front, this photo, from the last page of the "scrapbook," is probably from the 1920s or 1930s.)

CHAPTER 45

BELMONT, MISSISSIPPI

(Six pages...typed. Written in the "W.P.A. days" of the '30s)

Belmont, Mississippi, is in the extreme southern part of Tishomingo County, on the Birmingham Division of the Illinois Central Railroad, about ten miles from Red Bay, Alabama, on the east and forty-eight miles from Corinth, Mississippi, to the northwest. It is connected with the county site of Tishomingo County, Iuka, twenty-eight miles away, by a good graveled road, Mississippi State Highway Number 25, affectionately known as the John M. Stone Highway, named for Mississippi's beloved governor. This state highway long ago was the Eastport and Fulton road and connected what were, in pioneer days, two of the most important towns in northeast Mississippi – Eastport in Tishomingo County and Fulton in Itawamba County. Belmont is three miles from the Alabama state line and about five miles from the Itawamba County line.

It is the second town in Tishomingo County in size, having a population of about 700.

Belmont sits on a high ridge, or watershed, the waters of which divide, one side going to the Tombigbee River and thence to the Gulf of Mexico, the other to Big Bear Creek and on to the Tennessee River. The town has a particularly beautiful location. To the east is the narrow valley of Big Bear Creek, with immense ledges of sandstone rock, enough, it would seem, to furnish the entire State of Mississippi with building material. Beyond Bear Creek are the Freedom Hills, known as such because the mountaineers who inhabited these fastnesses are something of a law unto themselves, living as did their pioneer ancestors, resisting every so-called advancement.

Nearby are large deposits of minerals like limestone, sandstone, gravel, chert and asphalt.

Belmont was once in the midst of a great hardwood forest, but the giant Golden Saw Mill in Golden and the big mills in Tishomingo have almost denuded the country.

HISTORY

Long before the building of the Birmingham Division of the Illinois Central Railroad, completed in 1907, a settlement called Gum Springs sprang up where the town of Belmont now stands. Early citizens built the Gum Springs School House, several stores and then a post office called Belmont. By the time they planned the Illinois Central road through the southern part of Tishomingo County, a fair-sized country settlement had gathered, getting its freight from the nearest town, Iuka, nearly thirty miles away.

The completion of this Illinois Central Birmingham Division placed several rural settlements in Iuka's trade territory on the railroad. Not one was willing to give up its identity, so the railroad line was dotted with stations only a few miles apart. None could hope to grow into towns of any size. Belmont, next to the last stop in Mississippi, has grown to be the largest.

Belmont was incorporated by an Act of the Legislature signed by Governor E. F. Noel on January 22, 1908. The first officers appointed by the governor were: Mayor C. C. Shook. Marshall John H. Clark. Alderman: S. P. Beatty, Dr. R. L. Montgomery and Dr. E. F. McRae.

A civil engineer named Noel, from the Illinois Central Railroad, first platted the town.

The first bank in Belmont was a branch of the Tishomingo Banking Company of Iuka. That bank failed in 1912, and the Belmont branch closed its doors. A second bank started in 1913 but lasted only three years. The present bank opened its doors in 1919 and is one of the strong institutions of the state. During 1930-31-32, when banks all over the nation were closing daily, the two banks in Tishomingo County went through unscathed.

J. C. Clements operated one of the largest chicken farms in northeast Mississippi near here, but it no longer exists. Mr. Clements is devoting time to his large lumber mill.

There is one large, electrically-operated cotton gin.

Funds from the W. P. A. are helping construct a handsome City Hall and Community Center of concrete blocks that will be worthy of a town many times the size of Belmont. It will house a large auditorium capable of seating 500 to function for the mayor's court or other public gatherings, offices for town officials, a library and recreation room, plus rooms in the basement for a jail used for holding prisoners headed for the county jail. This building will cost about $12,000.00.

The town has twelve stores, two drugstores, a beautiful funeral home, two good cafes and three filling stations.

The hotel of Belmont serves the best of meals from a well-equipped brick building that exhibits the progressive spirit of Belmont.

The pride of the town is the handsome school plant with its accredited high school, a separate building for the primary grades, a fully equipped gymnasium and twenty-three teachers plus pupils. H. L. Shook serves as superintendent with a core of efficient teachers.

The town has three churches – Church of Christ, Methodist (an outgrowth of the Old Valley Methodist built across Bear Creek in pioneer days), and the Baptist (an outgrowth of Ebenezer, also a pioneer church). The Baptist Church, being rebuilt as a brick building with an auditorium seating at least 500, plus twenty Sunday School rooms, will soon be completed.

A 1928 bond issue has provided well-paved roads, the Tishomingo County Electric Power Association provides unbelievably cheap electricity and the town's drilling of a well will soon provide Belmont with water, sewage and all the modern conveniences.

Belmont has a flourishing Masonic Lodge, which owes its existence to an older lodge established in Itawamba County more than a half-century ago, a good newspaper called The Tri-County Weekly and a beautiful city park.

The town's present officers are: Mayor A. G. W. Byram. Alderman: C. E. Yarber, C. Cromeans, Ellis Wright, George Barnes and W. Cleveland.

CHAPTER 46

TISHOMINGO CITY – A BRAND NEW TOWN

(Miss Lyla kept a 16-page booklet, A Brand New Town, produced by the Tishomingo Townsite Company. It has a map in the back showing all the lots available in the new town of Tishomingo City. There is no date, but the booklet speaks of this NEW town being on the NEW Illinois Central Railroad, which places the publication date around 1908. The Townsite Company gives a brief history of the area and then focuses on plans and expectations for the future.)

TISHOMINGO CITY, MISSISSIPPI

"Tishomingo" is an Indian word meaning "brave warrior." The first white settlers, who came to North Mississippi before the Indians left the country, tell an interesting story of the Indian warrior "Tishomingo."

They relate that the very site where Tishomingo City is located was the scene of many bloody conflicts between the Tishomingo tribe and the war-like Seminoles, for the possession of the health giving springs of that section. In one of these fights, Tishomingo alone slew many of the Seminoles, among them being their Chief, and almost annihilated the entire tribe, thus gaining for himself the name of "Tishomingo" or brave warrior.

OFFICERS OF THE TISHOMINGO TOWNSITE COMPANY

A. J. Hackett – President
Gov. A. H. Longino – Vice President
J. J. Coman – Secty' & General Manager
S. J. Snook – Treasurer

BOARD OF DIRECTORS

J. C. Longstreet, Dr. F. T. Carmack, A. J. Hackett, A. H. Longino, S. J. Snook, J. J. Coman, P. E. Williams.

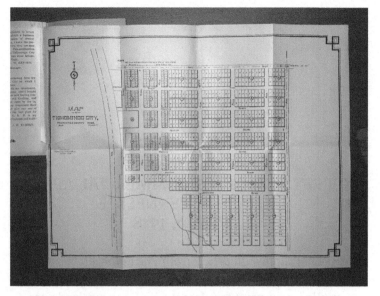

This foldout map in the back of the booklet shows the lots in
Tishomingo City.

*(After brief statements singing the praises of Farming Lands,
Timbered Lands, Manufacturing, Bank, Kaolin, Water Power,
Electric Railway and Health, the Townsite Company ends its
booklet with one last topic.)*

NOW IS THE TIME

To take advantage of the opportunity to buy a
cheap home on a new railroad, in a splendid farming
and manufacturing section where pure water and good
health abound.

CHAPTER 47

A YEAR OF WAR
EXCERPTS FROM THE COMMERCIAL APPEAL
(MEMPHIS, TENNESSEE)
APRIL 6, 1918

(Miss Lyla clipped an article from The Commercial Appeal [newspaper] on April 6, 1918. She chose to keep this now crumbling newsprint for almost a half-century and pass it along in her box of papers. A few selected sentences reveal an interesting mindset from a challenging time.)

Today, April 6, closes the first year of our war with Germany. While it may not be a joyous anniversary it ought to be a thoughtful one. In one year this country has done many big things. Some have been done well, and in those who have done their full duty, all praise and all honor.

However, for those things which have not been done during the first year of the war we, the 100,000,000 American people, have ourselves to blame. We ought to have been preparing to defend our peace during all the days of our republic.

The year of the war has brought home to us how badly we were organized and how uncorrelated were our energies.

We have 1,500,000 young men in the field. They have been well fed, they are now well clothed. The camps of this country have been put in order. The forces of discipline are already seen reflected in the faces of every boy who has been in the army more than six months.

The slouch of the foot and the stoop of the shoulders are gone.

It is good to look upon the full-chested, heel-to-heel, clear-eyed young men.

Good officers are finding themselves and poor officers are being found out.

And what of the second year of the war?

First, a determination to go forward at all costs and at all sacrifices.

The souls of the nation must get in touch. Those things which are not necessary for the war must be discarded for the things that are needful.

America must will to win this war and then enforce its will. And that will can be enforced by throwing the strength of the nation behind it.

There is no reason why we should be low-spirited, and being overjoyous might make us light-headed. So let us be serene, confident and determined.

And so this day, the end of the first year of the war, here is to the flag of our country, the symbol of liberty and justice, whose stars shall never be lowered in defeat.

CHAPTER 48

LAYING OF THE CORNERSTONE
IUKA PRESBYTERIAN CHURCH
SEPTEMBER 1925

*(A handwritten note on the back of the photograph says,
"Laying Cornerstone Iuka Presbyterian Church Sept. 1925."
The picture is stamped:*

*E. B. Simmons
Photographer
Iuka, Miss.*

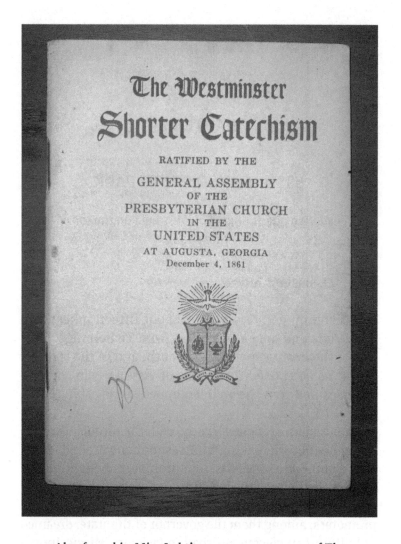

Also found in Miss Lyla's papers was a copy of The Westminster Shorter Catechism of the Presbyterian Church – December 4, 1861. Catechism is defined as "a summary of the principles of the Christian religion especially as maintained by a particular church in the form of questions and answers.")

CHAPTER 49

TISHOMINGO STATE PARK

(Typed, two pages, signed by Miss Lyla on the top of the first page)

Iuka, Mississippi July 24

Tishomingo State Park is about fifteen miles from Iuka and only a few miles from Tishomingo. It is one of the beauty spots of the South, and in the last few years, has attracted thousands of visitors who come to the park and rent the well-equipped stone cabins.

It is a place of rugged beauty, with the turbulent waters of Big Bear Creek making a horseshoe bend around. Long ago, a company of Mississippi promoters bought up the land with the idea of developing a stone quarry. They laid a rail line from the town of Tishomingo, and the promoters, among them the governor of the state, dreamed of building an electric railroad to Jackson, Mississippi, a dream never realized. For many years, the spot was just one of the forgotten, out-of-the-way places of the state.

Then the state geologist suggested that a spot of such rare beauty should be a park for the world to enjoy and appreciate. The county acted upon his suggestion and bought 700 acres and since then has added to it from time to time. There are now more than 1,500 acres in the park.

Designated for a CCC camp when a worldwide depression struck, the boys set into making the park an accessible place for future generations to enjoy. Skilled workers, under the direction of a master craftsman, produced handsome furniture, wrought iron chandeliers and attractive andirons for the Lodge. Stone cabins equipped with running water, shower baths, electricity for cooking and lighting, and every comfort they could devise attracted thousands during the summer months. Even in the dead of winter, the big Lodge, with the genial superintendent and family, became a destination for young people who came for dancing and other sports.

There is a swimming pool with lifeguards. A swinging bridge, built by the CCC boys, was for a long time an attraction but has lately been abandoned. Miles and miles of good gravel roads lead from one beauty spot to another.

According to botanists, the park contains a wide variety of wildflowers and shrubs. Among the unusual flowers is the southern yellow jessamine, which is supposed to grow in the wild only in the southern part of the state.

State geologist, Professor W. C. Morris, prepared a bulletin about the beautiful rock formations and grandeur. Some say there is enough sandstone within the park to supply building material for the entire state for more than a hundred years, but it has not been disturbed.

Tishomingo State Park is the abode of many wild animals and a place of beauty for the world to enjoy.

CHAPTER 50

IUKA MINERAL SPRINGS

(Three pages, typed on faded paper)

Iuka, Mississippi October 18

Nestling among the giant century-old forest trees in a grove of eleven acres beautified by both nature and man are Iuka's famous Mineral Springs. Within a space of less than a hundred feet are six springs, different yet alike in the priceless medicinal value given by the Great Healer for the aid of suffering humanity.

Where these springs originate, no one knows. Perhaps in the mountains of Kentucky or East Tennessee hundreds of miles to the north where as small streams they flow through one mineral after another, gathering as they come along the elements needed for the cure of many diseases and, after all have been gathered, coming to the surface in bold streams with every drop full of life-giving substances.

Scientists profess surprise that so many different streams should be found in such a small space, so different yet so vital. The springs contain sulfur, iron, magnesia, carbonic acid gas, alum and many other chemicals, suitable for so many ailments which mortals are heir, like stomach trouble, skin diseases, sore eyes, kidney trouble, nervousness, general debility and other disorders.

Photograph of The Iuka Mineral Springs Park taken from a copy of Wilmer Price's Illustrated Souvenir History of Iuka found in Miss Lyla's papers.

The waters from Iuka's Mineral Springs were awarded the Silver Medal at the St. Louis World's Fair in 1904.

The curative properties are:

SPRING NO. 1: Iron - good for chronic malaria, loss of appetite, anemia and general disability.

SPRING NO. 2: (The Beauty Spring) Good for dyspepsia, stomach troubles of all kinds and skin diseases. Red Sulphur. On account of the high sulphur content and other ingredients which help in clearing the body of impurities thus helping the complexion, it has always been known as "The Beauty Spring."

SPRING NO. 3: Iron and Magnesia. Called the Star Spring on account of the star-shaped concrete paving. A mild tonic; good for nervousness. A general favorite due to its agreeable taste.

173

SPRING NO. 4: Alum. Called "The Eye Spring." Tradition says that it was water from this spring that cured the eyes of Chief Iuka.

SPRING NO. 5: Black Sulphur. Good for Bright's disease and all afflictions of the kidneys, bladder and stomach.

SPRING NO. 6: White Sulphur – a milder sulphur with iron, potash and soda – good for stomach and skin troubles.

Nature has been most generous in providing these excellent springs amid such beautiful surroundings like the giant trees and the pretty winding creek, which finds its source nearby and is called Indian Creek because long ago the Chickasaw hunted and fished in its limpid waters as it flowed north to join the Tennessee River ten miles away. No wonder that in the middle of the nineteenth century, when the Memphis and Charleston Railroad was locating a town, this spot should be chosen over the more logical place at the crossing of the Eastport and Fulton road two miles east. Thus the city of Iuka was born.

Man too has done his part in making the park a thing of beauty, accessible to the traveling public. Substantial pavilions cover the springs where from pipes, the springs gush forth from the rocks. There are hundreds of native and imported shrubs and perennial flowers, great rustic ovens with an abundance of firewood and convenient tables for those who enjoy

Miss Lyla's Daughter
Elizabeth
August 1, 1917

174

dining in the great out-of-doors allure. For the lover of sports, there are tennis courts, croquet grounds, swings and other amusements. Adjoining the park is the baseball field where match games of softball and baseball are played in season, and between the park and field is the great transcontinental Highway, U. S. Number 72, which runs from New York to Los Angeles. Tourists by the thousands visit annually. They enjoy the breezes which reduce the temperature many degrees from town, drink the health-giving waters and carry away the memory of unusual beauty.

THIRSTY?—Still flowing in Iuka's Mineral Springs Park are the six sulphur and iron-laden springs which have made the site of Iuka famous for 400 years. Sampling the water are Harriet Ann Carmichael (1), Bobbie Sue Lomenick (2), Annette Reid (3), Shirley Sue Brown (4) and Patsy Lomenick (5).

Tradition and history meet in the park. Tradition tells that long ago, Indians far to the north, hearing of the spring near where the Tennessee River makes its turn to join the Ohio River, brought their sick and suffering to this spot. Here Iuka, the Chickasaw chief, was carried on a litter to be healed. Drinking the free-flowing waters cured him. Bathing his diseased eyes in the spring, which ever since has been called The Eye Spring, restored his sight.

In gratitude for his healing, he built his home where the Brinkley home now stands. Here he ruled his people, and in the town, he is buried. Tishomingo, the Warrior Chief, hearing of the restoration of Iuka, came to the place of healing waters and a great friendship sprang up between the chiefs who are honored in the names of the town and county.

When the first white settlers came to what later became Iuka, they placed hollow logs in the springs. One of these was recently removed and is in a fair state for preservation. Later the springs were enclosed in native rock with pipes, which prevented any possible surface contamination.

Many other legends are told of the springs also. History records that the land on which the springs are located was donated to the town by one of the first settlers of the county, David Hubbard, who with other family members, came to this county when it was first established and bought thirteen sections of land. By some means, the park became entangled with the Mineral Springs Hotel and was bought and sold for many years with that property until the town bought it about thirty years ago, and thus it became what it was intended to be - free to the world.

Only twice within the memory of man have the springs been exhausted. The first time was when Grant's army camped there. The second was when the Mississippi Power Company celebrated the entrance of hydroelectric power in the state and held a great barbecue there. It was attended by the governor and many high officials of the Power Company, along with more than half the entire county's population.

All public speakings are held there during the summer. In former years, the site held many religious observances. Here Sam P. Jones, the forerunner of most of the evangelists of this day, held one of his first revivals, converting many hundreds. Reverend Sam Steele, the writer of Creole Gumbo for the Commercial Appeal, preached here many times.

It is said that by drinking water from the Iuka Spring, Thomas A. Edison was nursed back to health after a severe spell of typhoid fever.

CHAPTER 51

IUKA RAILROAD YARD WITH THE
LEATHERWOOD HOTEL

*(Photo found in Miss Lyla's papers with a note handwritten
on the back)*

Part of a shipment of 17 cars of hardwood consisting of
ash – oak – gum – cypress and beech loaded at Iuka,
Mississippi, consigned to G. C. Gooch Logging Co. Memphis,
Tennessee. The logs came from W. H. Fairless' place
on Cripple Deer Creek – five miles east of Tishomingo,
Mississippi.

Photo of the first railroad station at Iuka, Mississippi
from a copy of the *Railway Employees Journal* – July 1938
found in Miss Lyla's papers.

CHAPTER 52

JEFF BUSBY

*(On February 15, 1934, in a speech to the U. S. House of
Representatives, U. S. Congressman from Mississippi, Jeff
Busby, proposed The Natchez Trace Parkway. It became
a reality.*
*Mr. Busby's speech is eight pages of tiny print. Two copies
were found in Miss Lyla's papers. The last four paragraphs
are included here as Chapter 52. It is interesting to note that
Jeff Busby attended the Iuka Normal Institute.)*

"As I look out toward the west from my office window,
I see the beginning of the Lee Highway here in Washington.
That beginning is the beautiful bridge that spans the
Potomac River. While that bridge is not more than one
half a mile in length, on it was expended more than
$15,000,000 – enough money to construct the Natchez
Trace Parkway from Nashville to Natchez, a distance of
500 miles.

The Lee Highway leading to the west out of Washington
connects Nashville with this Capital City. The construction
of the Natchez Trace Parkway would connect the southwest
with Nashville and the Lee Highway, thereby bringing
thousands of people hundreds of miles closer by highway
travel to the National Capital.

I commend this proposal to the Congress. I commend it to the administration. I submit that the construction of the Natchez Trace Parkway is one of the soundest, most permanent, and valuable investments that our Government could make.

I ask the cooperation of the Congress in the consideration and passage of the bills which I have proposed for the survey and construction of the Natchez Trace Parkway."

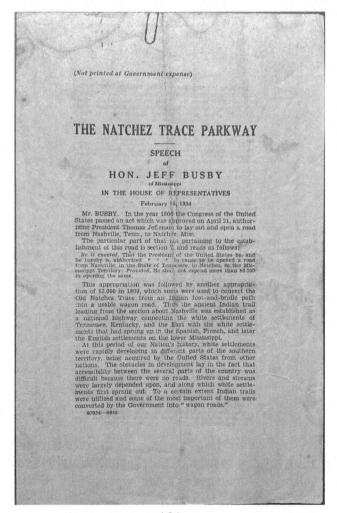

(Not printed at Government expense)

THE NATCHEZ TRACE PARKWAY

SPEECH
of

HON. JEFF BUSBY
of Mississippi

IN THE HOUSE OF REPRESENTATIVES

February 15, 1934

Mr. BUSBY. In the year 1806 the Congress of the United States passed an act which was approved on April 21, authorizing President Thomas Jefferson to lay out and open a road from Nashville, Tenn., to Natchez, Miss.

The particular part of that act pertaining to the establishment of this road is section 7, and reads as follows:

Be it enacted, That the President of the United States be, and he hereby is, authorized * * * to cause to be opened a road from Nashville, in the State of Tennessee, to Natchez, in the Mississippi Territory: *Provided,* He shall not expend more than $6,000 in opening the same.

This appropriation was followed by another appropriation of $3,000 in 1809, which sums were used to convert the Old Natchez Trace from an Indian foot-and-bridle path into a usable wagon road. Thus the ancient Indian trail leading from the section about Nashville was established as a national highway connecting the white settlements of Tennessee, Kentucky, and the East with the white settlements that had sprung up in the Spanish, French, and later the English settlements on the lower Mississippi.

At this period of our Nation's history, white settlements were rapidly developing in different parts of the southern territory, being acquired by the United States from other nations. The obstacles in development lay in the fact that accessibility between the several parts of the country was difficult because there were no roads. Rivers and streams were largely depended upon, and along which white settlements first sprang out. To a certain extent Indian trails were utilized and some of the most important of them were converted by the Government into " wagon roads."

40654—9843

181

CHAPTER 53

"THE FRIENDLY TOWN"

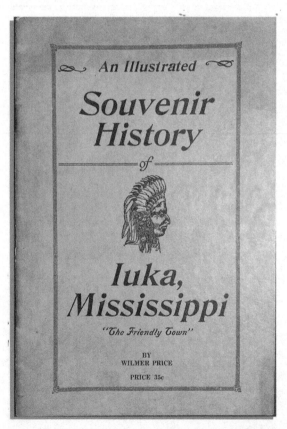

An Illustrated

Souvenir History

of

Iuka, Mississippi

"The Friendly Town"

BY
WILMER PRICE

PRICE 35c

(A copy of Wilmer Price's book, <u>An Illustrated Souvenir History of Iuka, Mississippi – The Friendly Town</u>, was found among Miss Lyla's papers.)

Samuel Wilmer Price, born in 1913, was the son of Webster and Adelaide Price of Iuka. He wrote his 18-page history in the 1930s. It has six chapters ranging from Indian Lore to the Battle of Iuka and contains several photographs like Woodall Mountain and Wilson Dam (on the Tennessee River). Wilmer Price died in 1940.

WILSON DAM
"An hour's drive from Iuka"
Photo from Wilmer Price's "The Friendly Town" an
Illustrated Souvenir History of Iuka, Mississippi

CHAPTER 54

DICK MERRILL PHOTO

(Henry Tyndall [Dick] Merrill was a celebrated aviator born in Iuka, Mississippi, who, among other feats, made the first trans-Atlantic round-trip flight in 1936. He was Miss Lyla's nephew. She kept a newspaper clipping but didn't mention the paper. Mr. Merrill's wife was actress Toby Wing.)

Wife, Son Welcome Merrill Home

Capt. Henry T. Merrill, famed trans-Atlantic flier and chief pilot for Eastern Air Lines, is welcomed home in Miami, Fla., by his wife, Toby, and son, Dick, after he helped a distressed EAL Constellation to a safe landing with 68 persons aboard at Bunnell, Fla. En route from New York to Miami, the plane threw a propeller which crashed through the side of the plane and killed Flight Attendant Gilbert P. Folz while cruising over the Atlantic 135 off the Florida coast. (AP Wirephoto.)

CHAPTER 55

WOODALL MOUNTAIN AND
OTHER HIGH POINTS

(A glimpse at Iuka and its surrounding area in 1936)

Iuka, Mississippi, is on the Memphis division of the Southern Railway, 115 miles from Memphis, Tennessee, and 200 miles from Chattanooga. It is six miles to the Alabama state line, sixteen miles to the Tennessee state line and eight miles to the nearest point on the Tennessee River. According to the government census of 1930, the town had a population of 1653. Because of the building of the Pickwick Dam, it is many hundreds more now.

Many old homes show the characteristic Southern architecture of "Befo' de War." Brick walks bordered with flowers lead to wide front steps. Broad square columns support the inevitable front porch. Beautiful hand-painted fan transoms and windows reaching to the floor with green shutters surround doors three inches thick and twelve feet high.

Iuka suffers less from the oppressive heat of mid-summer than any of the nearby communities, with the thermometer registering at least five degrees cooler than towns twenty miles away. The elevation of Iuka is nearly

600 feet, while at over 800 feet, the highest point in the state is four miles to the southwest.

These peaks are known locally as Woodall's mountains and are the foothills of the Appalachians. Protected in some measure by these hills to the southwest and the Tennessee River to the northeast, the town has been particularly fortunate in escaping the devastating storms that have ravaged other parts of the state. No major calamity has visited the town.

"Scene on Woodall Mountain – highest point in Mississippi, 3 1/2 miles from Iuka," from Wilmer Price's Illustrated Souvenir History of Iuka found in Miss Lyla's papers.

The surrounding county abounds in many kinds of minerals. The oldest formations of Paleozoic rocks in the state are found nine miles northeast of Iuka. Geologists have made special studies of the minerals of Tishomingo County, and the state geological department has issued many bulletins. The silica, sandstone, limestone, clays and asphalt deposits are practically inexhaustible. Tishomingo gravel is known throughout the United States as the best road-building material. Great mountains of this gravel are on the Lee Highway four and five miles east of the town, while smaller deposits are found all through the county. The shipping of gravel by freight has been the county's major industry ever since the Memphis and Charleston Railroad (now the Southern Railway) building in 1857. Hundreds of carloads are shipped monthly from the railroad mines by freight, with no records kept of the thousands of tons shipped by truck.

The hills of the county are particularly adapted to growing pine timber. While the virgin forests are practically exhausted, second-growth timber has been a source of considerable revenue to the farmer for many years. A few tracks of virgin timber are still untouched.

GOVERNMENT

A Mayor and Board of Alderman, consisting of five members, govern the town of Iuka. As stated before, it is the county site of Tishomingo County. Circuit Court is held here the first two weeks in January and the first two weeks in August. Chancery Court is held in June and December.

TRANSPORTATION

Railroads: The town is served by two trains each way daily on the Southern Railway, with through service to New York and Washington.

Air Service: An airport is in the process of being constructed 2 miles east of town off of Lee Highway, U. S. Number 72.

Highways: Lee Highway, U. S. Number 72, from New York to Los Angeles, is paved from four miles west of Iuka to Muscle Shoals and beyond, except for a stretch of about eight miles from the Alabama state line to Barton, Alabama.

Highways: John M. Stone Highway (Mississippi State Number 25) runs from the Tennessee state line to the Itawamba County line and is a good graveled road.

Taxis between any two points in the town proper, 25¢ fare.

ACCOMMODATIONS

Iuka has two hotels – The Leatherwood Hotel near the Southern Railway station and The Whitehurst Hotel on Eastport Street. Both serve meals from 35¢ to 50¢.

There are several good cafés in town.

Among the best of the town's boarding houses are the Whitten home on Main Street and the Bonds House on Pearl Street. Transients are sometimes taken in.

Tourist cabins are found about three-fourths of a mile east and west of town on the Lee Highway.

AMUSEMENTS

Iuka has only one motion picture house, The Majestic. Currently, there is no swimming pool – patrons going to Liddon's Lake near Corinth, Miss.

INDUSTRIES

Iuka and Tishomingo County are fertile fields for developing many varied industries. Hundreds of cars of gravel are shipped by freight and truck monthly from both public and private mines. The newer industry of mining lime and sandstone rock for building purposes employs many.

The lumber industry has been, through the years, a means of livelihood. Iuka is the most significant shipping point in the United States for 2 X 4 lumber. Also, the shipping of pulpwood for making paper is essential to the town's business.

ENVIRONS

Iuka is the hub of the tri-state area with Shiloh National Park and Pickwick Dam to the north, the government development at Muscle Shoals to the east, the city of Corinth and National Cemetery to the west and the CCC Camp on Big Bear Creek near the town of Tishomingo to the south.

Taking the John M. Stone Highway (Mississippi State Number 25) to the Tennessee state line and from thence over a Tennessee highway plainly marked, Pickwick Dam on the Tennessee River is nineteen miles to the north of Iuka. Shiloh Park is six miles further, while still further, crossing the Tennessee River over the beautiful toll bridge at Crump's Landing; one goes through farming country to the historic little city of Savannah. The Cherry Mansion overlooking the river is where Grant's headquarters were during the Battle of Shiloh.

189

Going east eight miles on U. S. Highway Number 72 to Riverton Junction and taking a good road north eight miles, one reaches the town of Riverton, where forty or more years ago, the building of Colbert Shoals Canal became the first of the government projects on the Tennessee River. Colonel Goethals, who later built the Panama Canal on the same plan, designed and built this canal. Riverton, at that time, was advertised in all the big newspapers and magazines as the upcoming city of the South, as it held the key to all-year navigation of the Tennessee River. The boom and prosperity were short-lived as the railway superseded river traffic leaving few boats on the Tennessee River to use the locks. Soon the town, already laid off in city lots with electrical lights and modern conveniences, resumed its old-time aspect of just a little river town, sleepy and uninviting. With the building of Pickwick Dam, the entire town of Riverton, with its locks and canal, will be flooded and become only a memory, as will the short-line railroad, built by an English capitalist named Parrish, scrapped a few years ago.

Going further east from Riverton Junction on the Lee Highway, one goes through the Tennessee Valley of north Alabama, famous in song and story for the many beautiful old Southern homes, some of which are visible from the Lee Highway. Thirty miles from Iuka is the town of Tuscumbia, Alabama, old long before Alabama became a state. Further is Sheffield, where the government, during the World War, built two immense nitrate plants. Still further is Muscle Shoals, famous for the immense power plant making and distributing electricity all over the South.

CHAPTER 56

NEW HISTORY WITH AN OLD SETTING

(These three typed pages, signed on the top of the first page by Miss Lyla, are probably part of a longer document, but our searches found nothing.)

Iuka, Mississippi May 1

New history with an old setting...New developments in primitive surroundings...History and development going hand in hand after a slumber of more than a hundred years. Such is the opening up of the Pickwick Dam area on the Tennessee River.

With the new development, interest in history revives, and this territory's role in developing the state is coming to light. Much forgotten; much never recorded. Pioneers were too busy making history and carving homes from the vast wilderness to write down the history.

Hardin County, the first county established in west Tennessee, is the location of Pickwick Dam. It was part of the Jackson Purchase and, because of its size, could well have been called the state of Hardin, since it extended from beyond the Tennessee River to the Mississippi River. That was short-lived, however, as west Tennessee developed rapidly after being opened up by the white men with the cession from the Chickasaw Indians. Soon this one large county was divided into Hardin, McNairy, Hardeman, Fayette and Shelby counties.

Colonel Joseph Hardin, the county's namesake, was a Revolutionary War soldier and friend of Tennessee's first governor, John Sevier. Governor Sevier gave Colonel Hardin the right to stake off 2000 acres in west Tennessee. Hardin and his family, seven sons and one daughter, traveled down the Tennessee River from their earlier home in the ill-starred state of Franklin. They arrived by flatboat with all their possessions, followed by four other families of about 26 persons to make the first settlement at the mouth of Horse Creek. Soon others arrived, building a courthouse, holding the first court session in west Tennessee at the new settlement called Hardinville and forming Hardin County on November 13, 1819.

By the 1830s, a new settlement on the River at Rudd's Ferry displaced Hardinville, and as other counties formed out of the original lands of Hardin County, the county site moved to the ferry settlement giving birth to Savannah. For 105 years, Savannah has been the beautiful capital of the proud old county. Though Rudd's Ferry is no longer there, the site is now known to visitors as the Cherry Home, where General Grant stayed during the battle of Shiloh. Much of the house's furnishings are as they were on that memorable day in April 1862. General Lew Wallace, another visitor to the home, later achieved great fame in the literary world as the author of Ben Hur and The Fairer God.

Across and up the river is Shiloh, the scene of one of the Civil War's bloodiest battles, which Bishop Gailer pronounced as the "first great battle on the American continent." Perhaps in no other battle did so many celebrities take part. Grant, W. T. Sherman, Don Carlos Buell, General Lew Wallace, Hurlbut, Prentiss, McClernand and others were on the Federal side. Confederates were Albert Sidney Johnston, General Leonidas Pope, John C. Breckenridge, General P. T. Beauregard and General William Hardee.

"Shiloh Military Park," from Wilmer Price's Illustrated Souvenir History of Iuka found in Miss Lyla's papers.

Others of lesser rank who attained distinction after the battle were James A. Garfield, later president of the United States and Robert G. Ingersoll, the great writer and thinker. On the Southern side were Isham G. Harris, governor of Tennessee, William B. Bate of Tennessee and Fighting Joe Wheeler of Alabama. On every National Cemetery today are found the stanzas of the immoral poem of Theodore O'Hara, The Bivouac of the Dead. The writer was engaged as a Confederate soldier in the battle.

Pickwick post office is said to have been named by an early settler who was a great lover of Dickens.

Not far from Pickwick Dam is White Sulphur Springs, which in the years before and immediately following the

Civil War was a famous watering place vying with the famous White Sulphur Springs in Virginia. Memphis capitalists owned and operated the springs and hotel. Wealthy pleasure-seekers from Nashville, Memphis and elsewhere engaged in fashionable balls, fox hunts and other sports during the summer. The old hotel remains as a mute reminder of better days.

A few miles away, Red Sulphur Springs is just off Mississippi Highway Number 25. This spring was a great watering place also, with the sulfur waters from the several springs so strongly impregnated as to be noticed many hundred feet away. These waters are of undoubted virtue in treating various skin troubles, and many people have sold their homes elsewhere and bought places where they could at all times have access to the springs. For a long time, Judge Jere W. Clapp of Memphis owned the hotel and springs and spent his last years there. A small hotel overlooking the springs now takes the place of the old hotel, which burned several years ago.

Many terrible tragedies have occurred in and around the Red Sulphur Springs Hotel. One of the worst was the killing by Gus Thomas of Dr. Murphy, a peacemaker who happened to be spending the night there. Dr. Murphy's body was placed in his buggy, where it was later found. Thomas was sentenced to life in prison but later escaped by swimming the Tennessee River.

Cook's Landing is in the adjoining county of Tishomingo in Mississippi, not more than twelve miles up the river from Pickwick. Many favored this spot on the river for the dam, but the idea was discarded because of unfavorable corings. Cook's Landing was the home of Colonel Marcus Cook in the days before the Civil War. Later he moved to Iuka.

CHAPTER 57

BERRY LEE MARTIN

(Tucked away in Miss Lyla's papers was a one-page clipping from the July 1938 edition of the Railway Employees Journal. She probably wrote this article announcing the retirement of Berry Lee Martin of Iuka. It certainly has a "Miss Lyla" ring to it. As a point of interest, Edwin Merrill, mentioned in the article, is Miss Lyla's father.)

MARTIN RETIREMENT STIRS MEMORIES OF HISTORIC IUKA, MISSISSIPPI AGENCY

Excerpts From

THE RAILWAY EMPLOYEES JOURNAL – July, 1938

BERRY LEE MARTIN

Brother Berry L. Martin was the third man to hold the job of station agent at Iuka. The original agent at this Mississippi point was John Marshall Stone, who served until he was elected state senator and went on to become Mississippi's governor for thirteen years. The second agent was Edwin Merrill, grandfather of aviator Dick Merrill.

Voluntarily retiring after fifty-six years of active railroad service with one company is the remarkable record of Brother Berry L. Martin, 75-year-old station agent for the Southern Railway in Iuka, Mississippi, and since December 9, 1922, a member of the Benefit Association of Railway Employees. Brother Martin's retirement was due to ill health and is regretted by the many close friends he has won in and about Iuka as agent in the town's historic station. Officials of the Southern are sorry to see him leave the job he has done so well and have not appointed his successor.

To old timers versed in the lore of this section, the resignation of Berry Martin brings to mind the fact that though the Iuka agency is eight-one years old, there have been but three agents, two of whose combined service extends over three-quarters of a century, a fact perhaps unequaled and certainly not excelled in the United States. Brother Martin's position in the Iuka office has come to be considered a lifelong job.

196

Following the Civil War, John M. Stone, a colonel of the regiment he organized, returned to Iuka and again took up railroad work. He served until he was elected state senator, from which place he went to the governor's chair for thirteen years.

During the years after the war, Stone had a clerk in the office who took up the work upon Stone's resignation. This was Mr. Edwin Merrill, whose interest in the work is illustrated by the fact that he served thirty-five years without a vacation. While Merrill was the Iuka agent, Rube Burrows, a notorious desperado of the era, and his gang of outlaws were making the lives of agents guarding the money of the railroad and express companies extremely hazardous. Pinkerton, the great detective, visited Iuka many times in search of the outlaws, who were at last captured.

It is said of Mr. Merrill, whose grandson is the noted aviator, Dick Merrill, that he attended to the office's business so closely that he was not seen on the streets of the town for more than fifteen years.

Learning telegraphy in its infancy, when the messages were taken on the old time instruments using ticker tape with the dots and dashes, Merrill never did teach himself to depend on

EDWIN MERRILL

197

his ears alone. He continued to use the outmoded devices. Some of these ancient instruments are now treasured for their historical value.

In 1898 Brother Berry Martin, then 35 years old, came to Iuka from Madison, Alabama. He was born in Madison and had been the agent there for ten years. When he took charge of the Iuka agency, troops were passing daily for the concentration camps at Fort Oglethorpe, Georgia, to go later to Cuba and participate in the Spanish American War.

Brother Martin has endeared himself to the public with his unfailing courtesy and efficiency and has earned, after many years of able service, the leisure he now enjoys.

CHAPTER 58

LETTER TO MRS. E. N. REED

(Built in 1871/1872, The Mineral Springs Hotel sat beside the railroad tracks in Iuka and "boasted the largest and finest ballroom between Memphis and Chattanooga." This grand hotel burned in 1944. The following letter, postmarked March 15, 1944, to Mrs. E. N. Reed of Iuka from Mrs. Ezekiel S. Candler of Corinth, Mississippi, provides some history of the hotel.

The letter is signed Ottie. That would be Zeke Candler's third wife Ottie Doan Hardenstein. Interestingly, Zeke's second wife was Effie Merrill Neuhardt, Miss Lyla's sister and the former wife of John Neuhardt, co-founder of the Iuka Normal Institute, who died in 1912. Effie Merrill Neuhardt Candler died in 1930. Also, Mrs. E. N. Reed would be Anna Lou Matthews Reed.)

Mrs. Ezekiel S. Candler
1022 Filmore Street
Corinth, Mississippi

March 15, 44

Dearest Luna

Your letter just rec. and always a joy to hear from you.

Zeke and I have grieved over the loss of the Iuka hotel and wish we could go up and see the ruins. Jake has gone back to Arizona – Couipl [sic] lives in Corinth – Loeta [sic] doesn't drive and no chauffeur – and no one else takes trips or drives that I know – on acct of Gas.

Zeke is sitting up this morning and goes back to bed in little while – he got out in the sun yesterday for an hour and hope he will consent to again today before he goes to bed – he is in bad shape – Dr. McRae says he has the same trouble that his Pa had before he died – called "Parkinson Disease" – loss of strength in legs – and nerves – and loss of strength.

Luna – Zeke says – his family landed in Iuka in July 1870 he says. A frame hotel was standing on the same spot of ground on which the Mineral Springs Hotel was built and it was built in 1871 or 1872 – the frame hotel having burned in 1870. The Mineral Springs Hotel was built by the Iuka Hotel Co. – of which Co. he thinks Mr. Hammerly was President.

The citizens took stock in the Hotel Co. in addition to the funds derive in that way. The Co. borrowed $5000 from a widow in Corinth (don't remember name) and gave her a first mortgage on the Hotel, and $5000 from Mrs. Harris, a widow in Iuka – and gave her a second mortgage on the Hotel. The Hotel Co. paid neither of them and Mrs. Harris to protect herself paid off the mortgage to the Corinth widow and acquired the hotel property under the mortgage she held and she sold it to Mayor R. H. Allen for $4500 not enough to reimburse her for the amt she paid the Corinth widow, who held the first mortgage. Mrs. Harris suffered a total loss of her loan and more. Mayor Allen after–

wards operated it for sometime but he gave a mortgage on it himself to old Col. Taylor's Bank in Corinth and he did not pay Taylor, and he had it sold and John Allen bought it (Congressman Allen) and he sold it to Capt. Watson for 15,000 and Dean and Neuhardt later bought it and ran the Iuka Normal Institute in it.

Have given you the history of the Hotel as Zeke remembered. Hope it will help Lila.

If there are any questions she wants to ask and he knows them – tell her to write him.

Zeke is calling and I must go – my pen is so bad – I hate to send this – but it is the best I can do today.

Come down when you can –

Love,

Ottie

CHAPTER 59

NATCHEZ TRACE

(This tattered, typed, three-page history of the Natchez Trace has a small portion torn from the corner of each page. Contents point to Miss Lyla writing it after WWII. She signed the top of page one.)

Iuka, Mississippi July 6

Would you like to put your hands on the steering wheel of your car and in a few minutes be driving along a good graveled road over one of the oldest roads in the world? Well, maybe you can by traveling through Lauderdale and Colbert counties in Alabama and certain counties in Mississippi on the Natchez Trace.

Archaeologists have made excavations that prove this is part of an old Indian trail that extended from Mexico to Canada long years before Columbus ever dreamed of crossing the ocean in search of a new route to India. Or even before Leif Erickson and his hardy Norseman ever touched the shores of Massachusetts and called it Vinland.

Be that as it may, there is much foundation for this supposition from the many relics uncovered from time to time. Historians know that the Natchez Trace, which followed an old Indian trail, was the first government constructed road in the southwest and was the forerunner of the many magnificent highways of today. As far back as 1794, this was a mail route over which John Swaney carried mail by horseback to the few white families who lived along the way. President Jefferson's administration appropriated $6,000 and built this highway from Nashville, Tennessee, to Natchez, Mississippi.

In 1801, by the treaty of Chickasaw Bluffs, the Indians conceded the right of way to the United States to lay out a road through their settlement from Nashville to Natchez. The Choctaws, by the treaty of Fort Adams, conceded the same right. This road was to cross the Tennessee River in what is now Tishomingo County at the mouth of Bear Creek, but the original survey found the expense of filling would be too great. George Colbert, a half-breed Indian, who lived a few miles upstream, suggested that the crossing be made at his place. Colbert Ferry became known to all the traveling public. Colbert made as much as $20,000 a year for the ferry privilege.

A few miles past Colbert Ferry, the Trace crossed Bear Creek at Stemini Ferry, kept by another Indian. Of Chief Stemini, we know little other than he had his home on the bluff, and like the other Indians who kept ferries, is supposed to have amassed a fortune in the collection of ferry charges. The fee was $1.00 per person, and if the passengers arrived at sundown, they had to spend the night at the tavern, for no Indian would cross the river after dark.

The name of Stemini is about forgotten, but the big Lee Highway bridge across Pickwick Lake marks where Stemini kept his ferry long ago over Bear Creek.

From Stemini Ferry, the road passed into Alabama to what was at one time called Underwood Village near today's Allsboro. The Tuscumbia D. A. R. years ago marked the spot with a handsome granite marker now in a wilderness and seldom seen. A few miles further, the Trace is the main road from Allsboro to Tishomingo, Mississippi. In the town of Tishomingo, the Trace is again marked with a granite marker erected by the Corinth Chapter, La Salle D. A. R.

ANDREW JACKSON AT THE HERMITAGE

A stately Andrew Jackson graces the front cover of a 52-page booklet entitled Andrew Jackson at the Hermitage compiled by Mr. Reau E. Folk. The booklet, found among Miss Lyla's papers, mentions no publisher or date.

Another of the stations in Tishomingo County was initially called Good Springs and should have been a place marked. In the early days of the 19th century, Andrew Jackson and his hardy Tennesseans, on their way to Horse Shoe Bend, camped there, and the patriotic citizens have ever after called the place Jackson's Spring. Relics found in the vicinity, are from both whites and Indians. Ancient Spanish coins, beads, iron cooking vessels and other things of interest to archaeologists show travel from many centuries ago. An interesting silver medal or religious insignia that no one understands, is a highly prized possession of a certain citizen. This abandoned spot and the Good Springs are almost lost.

According to the Natchez Trace Park Association, restoration work is under construction in many places in Alabama, Mississippi and Tennessee. The road will not always follow the original highway but will give the traveling public some idea of the early history of the South. In Lauderdale County, Alabama, grading work is now in progress at a cost of about $600,000, extending the road from the Tennessee state line to the Florence – Waterloo Road.

The first construction priority for Mississippi is the completion of the Parkway northward from Jackson, Mississippi, to Tupelo, where the Association has its headquarters, a distance of 164 miles. At the start of the last war, all construction stopped with some 83 miles of grading and minor drainage complete. Presently, 67 miles south of Kosciusko are being graded, leaving 67 miles with work yet to begin.

When finished, the right of way will average about 800 feet. The National Park Service will have charge of the protection and preservation of the Natchez Trace.

CHAPTER 60

WOMEN OF IUKA'S TWENTIETH CENTURY CLUB WIN NATIONAL "BUILD A BETTER COMMUNITY" CONTEST – 1950

(In her papers, Miss Lyla kept a copy of the May–June 1950 edition of The Mississippi Woman's Magazine.)

At the General Federation of Women's Clubs national convention in Boston, Mr. Joseph B. Hall, president of the Kroger Company, presents Mrs. Minor R. Nixon with the $10,000 top award.

The Mississippi Woman's Magazine

ATTEND BOSTON MEETING–Seven members of the Twentieth Century Club of Iuka attended the meeting of the General Federation of Women's Clubs in Boston. They are Mrs. K. L. Rushing (1) chairman of the improvement contest; Mrs. E. E. Cutshell (2), Mrs. Minor R. Nixon (3), retiring club president; Mrs. O. L. Gaineys, Jr. (4) secretary; Mrs. T. B. Collum (5), Mrs. J. E. Thomas (6), club reporter, and Mrs. P. L. Sweeney (7).

(Photo courtesy Commercial Appeal)

IUKA NUMBER

Vol. XXVI   May-June, 1950   No. 3

ATTEND BOSTON MEETING – Seven members of the Twentieth Century Club of Iuka attend the meeting of the General Federation of Women's Clubs in Boston. They are Mrs. K. L. Rushing, Mrs. E. E. Cutshall, Mrs. Minor R. Nixon retiring club president, Mrs. O. T. Gaines, Mrs. T. B. Collum, Mrs. J. E. Thomas club reporter and Mrs. P. L. Sweeney.

CHAPTER 61

DID YOU KNOW

(Miss Lyla kept a copy of the Iuka Rotary News from 1956 written by Ben McRae of Iuka. It appears that "Mr. Ben" verified his information through Miss Lyla.)

IUKA ROTARY NEWS – DECEMBER 11, 1956 (BEN MCRAE)

Iuka Rotary News – Editor (Ben F. McRae, Jr.)
December 11, 1956

Wayne Spinks, President
Harry Cosby, M.D., Vice President
R. A. McRee, Jr., Treasurer
Hiram A. Jones, Secretary

Our compliments to Brandon for his excellent talk on The Story of Our Time. Next up is Luke Robinson, and on Luke, too, we can depend on a good program.

Because we are bereft of any news of any nature, we have decided to make this our Historical Issue wherein we offer a lot of little facts about our vicinity which might be of interest to some of our newcomers. Most of these statements are verified by our friend and leading authority on local history, Mrs. T. M. McDonald.

Before the incorporation of Iuka, there was a post office hereabouts called Danton, Mississippi, which is believed to have been located about where the local colored cemetery is now. Serving as postmaster there in 1850 and 1851 was one John Robinson.

Eastport was a town long before Iuka, the town having moved here with the coming of the railroad. Eastport was incorporated in 1839, and Samuel DeWoody, great-grandfather of Louise Williams Cooper, was a mayor and owner of the hotel. The house now occupied by Mr. Dave Ables, just east of O. T. Gaines, is the only known house still standing which was moved here from Eastport.

There is some doubt as to whether Iuka was incorporated in 1856 or 1857, because the records in Jackson show the town's first mayor served from 1856 to 1858. His name was Demosthenes W. Davis and was, in addition to the mayor, an artist, Methodist Minister and our first postmaster. He was also editor of the town's first newspaper, The Mink.

Iuka's Mineral Springs were valued by the Indians for their healing qualities. The town site was used as an Indian burial ground, and at the time of incorporation, graves were visible everywhere.

The old wooden building located about where Cutshall Furniture Store now is, and which was removed not long ago, was Iuka's first post office and mayor's office and also served as a hotel.

Tishomingo County once included Alcorn and Prentiss County, too, with the county seat at Jacinto.

The Battle of Iuka, fought one-half mile southwest of town on September 19, 1862, is said to be, for the number engaged, the bloodiest battle of the Civil War. In a common grave near the colored cemetery, the spot marked by a State Historical Marker, lie 263 Confederate soldiers of General Sterling Price's command who died at the Battle of Iuka.

In 1882, Professor H. A. Dean and Professor John Neuhardt (brother-in-law of Mrs. T. M. McDonald) founded Iuka Normal Institute which was the first successful independent normal school in the South. This school, for both male and female, occupied the old Mineral Springs Hotel building and annex, and many of our older citizens now living received advanced education here.

A tannery and shoe factory was established here in 1882, but closed down after operating a year or two.

Slave galleries were once part of the sanctuary of the Methodist Church and were removed just before the turn of the century.

The first brick store building in Iuka was the one now occupied by Mrs. J. W. Hyatt. The bricks from the building are believed to have come from a kiln near what is now the Ed Kimberly home. It is known the bricks of our courthouse came from there. The second brick store was the Hyatt Building now occupied by Gallagher's Store.

The tall Monument in our cemetery marks the final resting place of the Honorable John Marshall Stone, uncle of Mrs. W. B. Fulkerson, and for 12 years governor of Mississippi. At the time of his death, Governor Stone was President of Mississippi A. & M., now State College.

He was head of the State Masonic organization and had been a colonel in the Confederate Army.

Iuka's first banker was Captain C. J. Hyatt, father of Bill Pyle's mother.

Iuka's Mineral Springs water won the Silver Award at the World's Fair in 1904. After this the town became quite famous as a resort, and the two large hotels and the annex, in addition to several other boarding houses, were kept full in summer for many years. Many people still living can remember the camp houses behind where Jourdan's Hardware now stands and the general camping area around the Jack Seward location where people who came from miles away in wagons to trade stayed overnight to break the trip. The hole in the pavement at the W. S. and T. L. Brown stores is caused by an old well which used to be there with oak trees around it.

The Presbyterian Church was once located near the present site of Jourdan's Planer and was moved over the railroad to its present location. Moving required about a week, and Sunday School was held en route. Looking back across the years, we wonder if our lives are very much different from those who came before us. We really doubt it because we strongly believe life in any age is about what we ourselves make out of it.

See you at Rotary.

"Service Above Self...He Profits Most Who Serves Best"

CHAPTER 62

MISS LYLA'S SPEECH

(In this speech, Miss Lyla did not indicate location or occasion, but from the subject matter and references made, it was probably in the early 1950s at the dedication of the Battle of Iuka Historical Marker on Highway 25.

Imagine Miss Lyla standing on the back of a flatbed truck, clutching a microphone stand, hat a bit off-center, paper in hand, speaking to a spellbound audience. Consider her words the very definition of Miss Lyla's Papers – a colorful history of Iuka, Mississippi, that Lyla McDonald researched, lived, told and wrote about for her entire life.)

****

I see from the Vidette that I am to make a speech. I have no speech to make but being one of the oldest native citizens of the town and always interested in the beginning of things, I have, through the years, accumulated data about the town and county.

We are grateful indeed to the Mississippi Historical Society and our young representative for accomplishing what we have long tried to achieve. Many years ago, the Thursday Club introduced a bill through our congressman to have the Iuka and Eastport battlefields recognized.

At that time, the federal government was marking the battlefields of the South, but Iuka and Eastport received no recognition. In the meantime, these historical spots have been almost obliterated, and the young people hardly know that where they unknowingly tread has been baptized in blood.

Historians have long disputed De Soto's wanderings in Mississippi. Some claim that he visited what is now Tishomingo County, and it was at the mouth of Bear Creek, where he gazed upon the Tennessee River, that the Indians told him of the greater river to the west to which he went and discovered the Mississippi River at Chickasaw Bluffs, now Memphis.

Long before the whites kept any records and when South Carolina still claimed this part of the state, there was a trace or trail from the far northeast to the far southwest by way of the crossing at the mouth of Bear Creek. This trail was The Mountain Leader's Trace, named for the famous Indian, Piomingo. There were only two ways to reach the southwest at that time: by coming down the Ohio River to the Mississippi or by this lonely trace, a mere bridle path through an unbroken wilderness where post riders carried government mail to the few whites. Two of the male carriers of that day were John Lee Swaney, whose mother was the sister of Richard Henry Lee, and John Donnelly.

When the Mississippi Territory was formed in 1798, the Indians gave the right to cut and open a wagon road between Nashville and Natchez. This road, laid out in 1802, became known in song and story as The Natchez Trace, which runs through the county from east to west. The engineers moved the original river crossing at the mouth of Bear Creek 16 miles upstream to where George

Colbert kept a ferry. He was said to have made $20,000 a year in ferry tolls during the rush to the west. Thieves, robbers and murderers of all kinds infested The Natchez Trace, chief among them were Big and Little Harp, Joseph Hare, and worst of all, John A. Murrell, who killed just for fun, gleefully throwing his victims into the river and riding off to kill again. There were not only thieves and murderers found along the Trace, but also many whose names we remember with pride, among them Davy Crockett, Andrew Jackson's men on the way to fight the Creeks, Philip Nolan, the man without a country and the eccentric Lorenzo Dow and his wife Peggy who made his church appointments two years ahead. The Trace crossed Bear Creek at Stemini Ferry, where the magnificent Lee Highway bridge is now. From Stemini Ferry, the road led to Allsboro, Alabama, then to Tishomingo, Mississippi and New Site. Someday this old road will be a National Park from Natchez to Nashville.

In the early days of the 19th Century, Eastport at the mouth of Bear Creek was a flourishing town of wealth and culture with a female college that taught all the arts of that day, fine needlework, painting, hair making, music plus Latin and Greek. There were about 20 stores, a bookstore, tinners, boot makers, Methodist and Baptist churches, a Masonic Lodge, a hotel called The Mansion House and a warehouse large enough to hold all the merchandise which was to be distributed all along the way to Aberdeen, Columbus and intermediate points. In its beautiful location at the head of all-year navigation on the Tennessee River, it was the rival of Memphis on the Mississippi. Both towns were started about the same time and incorporated within a few years of each other. The town on the Mississippi grew into one of the foremost cities of the U.S.; the other became a memory, only coming into notice with the building of the cottages by the Memphis syndicate.

A stage line ran from Eastport to Memphis. It passed just north of where Iuka was later built, thence to Burnsville, where it turned north into Tennessee, passing through the towns of Bolivar and Somerville, the same route that Highway No. 64 follows now. Early settlers told pitiful tales of the hardships of travel in those days when the driver sat on a high seat unprotected from rain, hail and snow. Certain points were designated for the change of horses. They tell of a driver who, on one of the coldest days of one of the coldest winters, failed to come down when the coach reached the station. Upon examination, they found him frozen with the lines in his hands, which had to be pried apart to release them. He was carried into the inn, and everything possible was done to revive him but without avail. Faithful unto death is an unsung, unrewarded hero whose name is unknown. Evidence of this old stagecoach road could be seen until a few years ago when the plow finished its work of destruction.

The stringing of one of the first telegraph lines in the world occurred over Tishomingo County's hills and hollows. S. F. B. Morse, after many heartbreaking failures, finally perfected the telegraph and received from Congress an appropriation to construct a line from Baltimore to Washington. Soon after, a line was built from Washington through Virginia, through Tennessee, thence to Tuscumbia, Alabama, Iuka and Jacinto, which at that time was the county site of Tishomingo County. From Jacinto the line extended into Memphis. There are many funny tales of the early days of that telegraph line. Tishomingo County had never within the mind of man had a drought. Season following season, harvests were plentiful, but a severe drought struck the county in the first year of the telegraph line. Crops that had looked so promising began to sicken and die. Farmers saw all their work going for nothing. Real suffering stared them in the face. Believing that the electric wire which passed overhead was parching their land, the farmers armed themselves with axes and blades and proceeded to cut down the wires. They demolished many miles before being stopped.

Tishomingo County was born from the lands ceded to the U. S. by the Treaty of Pontotoc when the Indians agreed to give up their homes and the graves of their dead and move to the land the government had provided for them in the west. There was no sadder page in history than this migration when they went over the Vale of Tears.

The county was named for the chief who was next to the king. Tishomingo means Warrior Chief, an appellation he received for his prowess in battle. We are indebted to Chief Tishomingo and the Colberts for saving the early settlers from extinction when Tecumseh tried to incite the Indians against the Americans in the War of 1812. Tishomingo's home was said to have been at old Carrollville near Baldwyn, Mississippi. He lived there 96 years before going with his tribe to the west, where he died in Little Rock of smallpox. Tishomingo was a friend of George Washington who gave him a medal and a small annuity.

Tradition says that Chief Tishomingo and Chief Iuka were great friends and often exchanged visits. One of the tales told by early settlers was of a white man on his way from his home to Tuscumbia who fell among thieves, as did the man in the Bible. They robbed him of his clothes and money and left him to die by the roadside. Tishomingo's son-in-law, Tombigbee, found him and took him to the chief's house, where he was nursed back to health. An escort then took the man to Chief Iuka where he was cared for and sent to his destination.

Where Iuka came from, tradition is silent, but through the years the story has come down that in his faraway home, he heard of the healing waters near the mouth of Bear Creek. Old, sick and with weak eyes, he was taken to this place on a litter. There his health was restored. Bathing his eyes in the alum spring, his eyesight improved, and afterward he stayed, living the rest of his life near the springs. His home was thought to be where the Brinkley home now stands.

Engineers surveying the Memphis and Charleston Railroad gave the chief's name to a new settlement that sprang up near where a post office called Danton had earlier been established. Iuka was born. There was also a Methodist Church nearby, which belonged to the Eastport circuit. One of the church's early pastors was Reverend M. H. Wells.

When it became known a town was to be built here near the Memphis and Charleston, enterprising citizens of Eastport bought land from the Hubbards and Usserys, who had come to the area soon after the county formed. The citizens established The Iuka Townsite Company, composed of Dr. Ben Hodges, Colonel Cal Terry, A. T. Matthews, Colonel Winston Price and others. The company sold lots, and people began building new houses.

A flourishing female college with well-trained teachers was established on the grounds donated by David Reeder Hubbard. His father (also named David) gave the town the gift of the mineral springs with the provision that the waters would be free to the town's citizens forever.

In early years, the Mineral Springs Park attracted visitors from all over the South, and Iuka became known as one of that day's most famous watering places.

The Memphis and Charleston Railroad was an outgrowth of many railroads, some of which were the first roads built in the U. S., among them the South Carolina. In the early days, a road was built from Tuscumbia called the "Tuscumbia, Courtland and Decatur Road." The first trains used horses, and later, when the line bought a locomotive, its first engineer was Jack Lawson, who had been a passenger on Stevenson's first steam locomotive in England.

Soon there were other lines, notably the Memphis and La Grange Road. By 1850, the Memphis and Charleston came into being after buying or leasing these older roads. The roads from the east and west joined in Iuka about 300 feet from where the depot now stands. In its near century of existence, Iuka never had such a celebration as it did that day, March 27, 1857. A golden spike marked the completion of the roads, and a distinguished gentleman whose name has been forgotten was given the honor of driving the spike. Toasts were drunk in something stronger than spring water, and when the time came to strike, he was unable to hit the spot. Turning to one of the ditch diggers who stood by, he asked, "Pat can you drive that blamed spike?"

Pat replied, "Faith and begorry, I'm the very man who can do it." To the humble ditch digger fell the honor of completing the road.

Many amusing tales have come down through the years of that celebration when the first whistle of the first locomotive came into town. Services were being held in the Methodist Church. The entire congregation ran out on the preacher and left him preaching to empty pews. When the free ride on the first train was well underway, a woman remembered that she had left her bread to rise. Realizing that it might be running all over the floor, she pulled the bell cord and ran every step of the way back to town to rescue her dough. Also, one housewife's cows persisted in grazing on the railroad right-of-way. Seeing her cows killed one by one, she soaked the rails with her homemade soap, causing the wheels to spin. This gave the cows ample time to get off.

The War Between the States coming so soon after the town was built blasted many hopes of a big flourishing city, but even with the war clouds gathering, many handsome homes and two churches were built. The Methodist still stands today, but the Baptist burned and the location changed.

Fine hotels were built, one of which stood at the Park's west gate entrance. This was known as the Wiggs House. Another was built on the hill to the southeast where Mr. Leslie Moser's home is now. This was the Cayce Hotel. The Blythe Hotel, which was burned by federal troops during the War Between the States, was where the present Leatherwood Hotel now stands, and a large hotel, The Iuka Springs Hotel, was built on the railroad where the brick hotel, The Mineral Springs Hotel, burned a few years ago stood.

The Mineral Springs Hotel was one of the finest hotels between Memphis and Chattanooga. The ballroom and good bands attracted the young people of wealth from Memphis and elsewhere. By some mistake, the springs became a part of the hotel property which caused the

219

town in later years much trouble until the town bought them in a bond issue with the first electric light plant.

The Civil War history of the town and county would have been endless had it been preserved, but the southern people who lived through tragic years were so anxious to get all of those days out of their minds and rebuild their shattered lives that little has come down by word of mouth of those perilous times. Being in the line of contending forces, the town and surrounding country were first in the hands of the Confederates, then the Federals. Iuka was the scene of one of the bloodiest battles considering the time of the engagement. The actual conflict took only about two hours, yet between fifteen hundred and two thousand men were killed or wounded in that time. A minie ball struck General Henry Little of Maryland through the head just as he advanced to receive instructions from General Sterling Price, the commanding officer. Colonel Celeus Price, son of the commander, caught General Little as he fell from his horse, mortally wounded. General Little was buried in the garden at the home of Major Coman in Iuka. Nearly all the homes in the town, the schoolhouse, boarding house, churches and hotels were used as hospitals for the wounded on both sides. The Federal dead were buried back of the schoolhouse and boarding house until after the war when they were carried to Corinth and reinterred in the National Cemetery. The 263 Confederate dead were buried in a trench in the Shady Grove Cemetery.

We are proud to have a marker on the highway showing those who pass by that we are not unmindful of what has gone before and are looking to better things in the future. We place this marker as one of the historical spots of Mississippi and of the South.

CHAPTER 63

TOM AND LYLA

Miss Lyla and her husband, Tom, on the front porch of the McDonald Home. Billie Burke Thomas found the negative of this photograph in the box of Miss Lyla's papers. In January 1991, Billie Burke had it developed. The date of the original snapshot is probably the 1950s.

"The present history of the town and county is for younger people to make and preserve for other generations. The early history has been colorful and worthy of emulation and to the coming generation a challenge and inspiration."

Lyla McDonald

222

APPENDIX

Chapter 19 Excerpt

STUDENTS AT THE IUKA FEMALE INSTITUTE 1859 – 1860

(The original pages, seen in Chapter 19, containing this list of names are in Miss Lyla's handwriting. It would be interesting to know the occasion for the list because the Data gives information from a time that is certainly later than when these young ladies were students in 1859 – 1860.)

Lists of students of the Iuka Female Institute
Sept 1859 – June 15, 1860

Names	Data	Residence
Antimesia Atkins	married Atkins	McNairy, Tennessee
Ellen Allen		Iuka
Sophronia Armstrong	Dead	Iuka
Nancy Armstrong		
Virginia Armstrong		
Lizzie Akers	married Jns Bromches	Tishomingo
Jack Ann Akers	married Walker	Tishomingo
Belle Barrett	married Daniel	
Julia S. Cook	married Nolen	Iuka
Sallie Coman	single	Iuka
Margaret Coman	married Alexander	
Rebecca Coman	single	Iuka
Endocia Conrsey	Lawrence Fowler	Iuka
Ophelia Conrsey	single	Coleman Co., Texas
Juliette Conrsey	single	
Laura Conrsey		
Annetta Conrsey	married Edmondson	
Georgia Castleberry	Walmsley	
Lucinda Coburn		
Ellen Coburn		
Hannah Cochran		
Malinda Cochran		
Virginia Dean	married Tom Akers	
Billie McIntosh	Dan Coleman	
Laura J. McIntosh	Mr. Hooks	

Mattie McIntosh		
Willie McIntosh	Daniels	
Linda J. McKnight	J. B. McKinney	
Mattie McPeters		
Ann McKinney		
Fannie McCrummon	Colonel Dowd	Smithville
Alice McCrummon		
Maggie McCorkle		Henderson Co., Tenn.
Sallie Moore		
Denton Pruitt		
Alice Mann	Martin Williams	Allsboro, Alabama
Florence Matthews	A. Castleberry	
Mattie Meeks		McNairy Co., Tenn.
Lizzie Moulton	McSehie	
Sarah Morris		
Mary T. Price	Captain Hyatt	
Mattie Purdy	O'Neil	
Mary Eliza Pickett		
Isabella Richardson		Panola Co., Miss.
Helen Ross		Henderson Co., Tenn.
Ester Smith		Cherokee, Alabama
Florence Smith		
Josie Stamps		
Lou Sargent		
Bettie Settle	Jns. Williams	

Chapter 28 Excerpt

STUDENTS AND TEACHERS OF THE IUKA FEMALE INSTITUTE – OCT 1870

Iuka Female Institute – J. E. Douglass
Oct. 1870

Sarah Tremble
Agnes Trimble
Annie Hatch
Carrie Douglass
Debbie Simmons
Mattie Matthews
Jimmie Doran
Fannie Doran
Mattie McCutcheon
Mattie Davis
Laura Worley
Annie Worley
Alice Worley
Nannie Davis
Lula Bowers
Gillie Bowers
Mattie Price
Clara Foote
Lucie Holloman
Cornelia Johnson
[sic] Telfair
[sic] Ricks
Hattie Sturdivant
Alice Holmes
Ada Millsaps
Mattie Deardolph
Effie Merrill
Belle Moss
Sallie Hammerly
Dixie Matthews
Hattie Hubbard
[sic] Allen
Mattie Kay
Lula Whitfield
Mary Ware
Mattie Clement
Agnes Castleberry
Ada Pulliam

Isabella Kenney
Jennie Ross
Alice Simmons
Bettie Box
Mollie Reeves
Ida Hudson
Willie Hendley
Smithie Hendley
Mamie Houston
Birdie Reno
Viola Henson
Lucy Payne
Alice Millsaps
Sallie Hubbard
Watt Tremble
May Cochran
Lizzie Cochran
Eddie Drake
Eva Grigg
Hattie Watson
Rachael Johnson
Hellen Alley
Effie Wadley
Sallie Millsaps
Marcella Bates
Allie Bates
Annie Harris
Fannie Seward
Dorthula Davis
Alma Tyler
Maggie Clark
Fannie Johnson
Sallie McCalla
Mollie Robinson
Susan Autrey
Miles Simmons
Ora Johnson

Chapter 29 Excerpt

CATALOGUE FOR THE IUKA FEMALE INSTITUTE
SCHOOL YEAR 1874-75

CATALOGUE

OF THE

Iuka Female Institute,

Iuka, Miss.

For the Scholastic Year ending June 16, 1875

FACULTY

Rev. J. E. Douglass, D. D.,
President, and Professor of Moral and
Mental Sciences, and Ancient Languages

Miss Bettie A. Hunt,
Teacher of Mathematics, French,
Natural Science, and Composition.

Mrs. E. A. Neblett,
Teacher of Natural Sciences,
English Grammar, Geography,
and Composition

Miss Amanda Sinclair,
Preparatory Department.

Mrs. F. E. Steger,
Music Department

Miss Bettie A. Hunt,
Art Department.

Names of Pupils

Alexander, Innis	Iuka, Miss.
Anderson, Jimmie	"
Autrey, Annie	"
Adams, Vic	"
Aydlett, Lula	Tuscumbia, Ala.
Barton, Lela	Iuka, Miss.
Barton, Joanna	"
Bates, Alice	"
Barbee, Anna	Germantown, Tenn.
Beck, Anna	Iuka, Miss.
Bevill, Georgia	"
Bevill, Jimmie	"
Blanton, Mary	Olive Branch, Miss.
Blythe, Ida	Iuka, Miss.
Bowdre, Lou Lee	Senatobia, Miss.
Castleberry, Agnes	Iuka, Miss.
Choate, Lucy	"
Copeland, Sallie	Olive Branch, Miss.
Crutchfield, Mollie	Longtown, Miss.
Darrett, Agnes	Como, Miss.
Davis, Mollie	Iuka, Miss.
Davis, Callie	"
Davis, Nannie	"
Dean, Della	"
Dean, Dixie	"
Doan, Allie	"
Dean, Sallie	"
Dean, Belle	"
Deardolph, Mattie	"
Driver, Alice	"
Dugger, Mattie	"
Ellis, Susie	"
Ellis, Lillie	"
Ellis, Ella	"
Evans, Lillian	Moscow, Tenn.
Evans, Alliene	"
Fisher, Benie	Longtown, Miss.
Foster, Eugenia	Memphis, Tenn.
Fowler, Ella	Tullahoma, Miss.
Ganong, Nelsie	Iuka, Miss.
Ganong, Willie	"
Gann, Alice M.	"
Gilbert, Priscilla	Iuka, Miss.
Gilchrist, Lula	Como, Miss.

Goyer, Ida	Iuka, Miss.
Grayson, Ora	"
Hammerly, Sallie	"
Hammerly, Mamie	"
Harris, Celeste	"
Hart, Mollie	"
Hart, Fannie	"
Haynes, Mattie	"
Hill, Jennie	Moscow, Tenn.
Holloman, Maude	Iuka, Miss
Holloman, Lucy	"
Hubbard, Sallie	"
Hubbard, Laura	"
Hughes, Annie	"
Hutchinson, Mary	"
Hyatt, Annie	"
Hyatt, Alice	"
Johnson, Cornelia	"
Johnson, Bettie	"
Langfrey, Jennie	
Lusby, Bettie	Peters' Land'g, Ark.
Lyles, Mary	Early Grover, Miss.
McCaula, Sallie	Iuka, Miss.
McClain, Annie	"
McMahon, Laura	"
Mackey, Azada	"
Mackey, Susan	"
Marshall, Mary	"
Massey, Etta	"
Massey, Josie	"
Massey, Allie	"
Massey, Lou	"
Massey, Mary	"
Matthews, Dixie	"
Matthews, Anna Lou	"
Miller, Sallie	Bledsoe's L'd'g, Ark.
Mitchell, Beulah	Longtown, Miss.
Merrill, Effie	Iuka, Miss.
Merrill, Helen	"
Moss, Molli	"
Mullins, Matilda	"
Mullins, Pattie	"
Nance, Fannie	"
Neblett, Ruth	"
Neblett, Ada	"
Paine, Ida	"

Parkinson, Mildred	Longtown, Miss.
Powell, Emma	Iuka, Miss.
Powell, May	"
Rice, Ervie	"
Rice, Zenia	"
Rice, Addie	"
Rice, Ida	"
Ringold, Mary	"
Ringold, Laura	"
Rowles, Alice	"
Rowles, Mary	"
Rowles, Maggie	"
Seay, Eva	"
Simmons, Virginia	"
Shands, Jessie	Senatobia, Miss.
Shelton, Frankie	Iuka, Miss.
Shelton, Lelia	"
Steele, Mary E.	"
Stephens, Sophia	"
Stephens, Addie	"
Stephens, Mary	"
Sturdivant, Hattie	"
Swansey, Ida	"
Taylor, Ida	Bledsoe's L'd'g, Ark.
Tepe, Anna	Iuka, Miss.
Tepe, Gertrude	"
Tepe, Ella	"
Thacker, Mollie	"
Wadley, Effie	"
Wadley, Mamie	"
Wadley, Julia	"
White, Rosa	Como, Miss.
Whitfield, Lula	Iuka, Miss.
Worley, Laura	"
Worley, Anna	"
Worley, Alice	"
Worley, Katie	"

TOTAL   131.

Studies

PREPARATORY DEPARTMENT
Speller, Webster's
Readers, McGuffey's Series.
Geography, Mitchell's Series

Arithmetic, Written, Ray's Series.
Mental, Colburn's
English Grammar, Butler's and Hervey's

COLLEGIATE DEPARTMENT

ENGLISH BRANCHES

Quackenbos' Natural Philosophy.
Youman's Chemistry.
Woods' Object Lessons in Botany.
Coming's Physiology.
Olmsted's Astronomy.
Peterson's Familiar Science.
Barber's Geology.
Algebra, Davies'.
Geometry, Davies'.
Trigonometry –Plane, Analytical, Spherical, Davies'.
Quackenbos' Rhetoric
Elements of Mythology.
Steven's History of the United States.
Mitchell's large Geography.
Monteith's Physical Geography.
Smith's Etymology.
Quackenbos' Composition.
Hedges' Logic.
Rivers' Moral and Mental Philosophy.
Political Economy, Wayland.
Kames' Elements of Criticism.
Alexander's Evidence of Christianity.
Parsing – Pollock, Young, Milton.

LATIN

Spencer and Bullion's Grammar.
Reader.
Caesar.
Virgil.
Cicero.
Horace.
Arnold's Latin Prose Composition.

FRENCH

Fasquell's Course
Introductory.
Grammar.

231

Conversation.
Telemaque.
Corinne.
Racine.

Charges

PER SESSION OF TWENTY WEEKS – HALF IN ADVANCE

BOARDING SCHOLAR – –

Board and Tuition – $100.00
Music, extra – 30.00
French – 10.00

DAY SCHOLARS –

Preparatory Department – 15.00
Collegiate, – 25.00
Music, extra – 30.00
French, extra, – 10.00
Ornamental, – 15.00 to 25.00

General Remarks

Boarders must furnish their own toilet; also a pair of blankets, sheets and pillow slips. On all clothing and bedding the name of the owner must be distinctly marked. Tuition in the literary department free to all ministers who are regular pastors.

BOARD OF INSTRUCTION.

On the Teachers depend the character and reputation of the Institute. Convinced of this, we have spared neither pains nor money in the selection of the Faculty. None but those of skill and experience have been, or will be, employed in the Institution.

MODE OF INSTRUCTION.

In many schools the primary object seems to be to crowd the mind with facts in Geography, History, Philosophy, etc., which the development of the intellectual powers is wholly overlooked. This system we repudiate. To teach the student to think, to reason, to compare, to judge – in a word, to develop the powers of the mind – will be the constant aim of the Faculty.

PHYSICAL EDUCATION.

To encourage the most enlarged and enlightened views of physical education, the Institute has been furnished with spacious out-grounds, where every variety of judicious exercise can be taken. In this department no pains will be spared to render the hours devoted to physical exercise both profitable and inviting. As much variety as possible will be sought. All innocent recreations and amusements which have a tendency to exhilarate the spirit and restore the elasticity of the mind, will be encouraged.

MUSIC DEPARTMENT.

Our intention is to make this department, as well as every other, answer the expectations of our patrons. In it will be employed none but Teachers of the highest qualifications. Every facility will be afforded the student of acquiring a practical as well as a theoretical knowledge of this useful accomplishment. This department is furnished with instruments of the best kind. Special instruction will be given in vocal music to all who desire it.

MODERN LANGUAGES

A knowledge of the Modern Languages is now regarded as an indispensable part of a polished education, and we have accordingly determined to keep at the head of this department a Teacher thoroughly qualified for this position.

GOVERNMENT

The utmost kindness will ever characterize our system of government. The leading objects of school government are good order and attention to study; and to secure these among our students, we depend more upon appeals to their sense of

233

propriety and pride of character than their fear of punishment.

GRADUATION

A diploma conferring the honors of the Institution will be given to those young ladies who shall pass a satisfactory examination in the Course prescribed. To those who complete the regular English Course, the degree of Mistress of English Literature will be awarded. To those who complete the Classic in connection with the English Course, the degree of Mistress of Arts will be awarded.

SESSIONS
AND
VACATIONS.

The scholastic year is divided into Sessions of twenty weeks each. Fall Session opens first Monday in September, and continues twenty-one weeks. The Spring Session opens the last Monday in January, and continues twenty weeks. No vacation will be given until the close of the scholastic year, except one week during Christmas, included in the Fall Session term.

GENERAL REGULATIONS

1. No student will be permitted to enter the Collegiate Department under twelve years of age, and then she must have a correct knowledge of the preparatory studies.
2. Students are admitted at any time, and charged from the week of entrance, inclusive. But those who delay their return, and permitted to advance with their classes, will be charged for the whole Session; and no deduction will be made for absence, except for sickness protracted one month, and then one-half of the charge will be returned or deducted.
3. No student will be admitted for less time than one Session, or the end of the current term.
4. Students are not permitted to take lessons of any kind out of the Institute on subjects taught in it, except by the special permission of the President.
5. Every student is required to be present at the opening and closing exercises, and deport herself with becoming respect and propriety.
6. Monthly reports will be sent to parents and guardians

234

to advise them of the attendance, deportment, and scholarship of their daughters or wards.

7. Attending parties, or places of public amusement, and holding communication, written or verbal, during the Session, with gentlemen, except near relatives, are found to be prejudicial to success in study, and often result in evil consequences, and are therefore strictly forbidden. In fact, all letters will be subject to the inspection and revision of the Teachers, if necessary.

8. Boarding pupils are placed under the charge of the President, who provides for them in the regular boarding-house connected with the Institute; or, when it is thought best, obtains board in private families, and thus keeps them all subject to the same regulations.

LOCATION

The Institute is located in Iuka, Mississippi, one hundred and fifteen miles east of Memphis, on the Memphis and Charleston Railroad, in one of the most healthy portions of the South. The excellent mineral waters, almost in the center of our town, attract large crowds during the summer months. Students from miasmatic regions are restored to perfect health by our pure atmosphere and mineral water. Many who, when they came, were scarcely able to walk to our springs, are now perfectly well. The citizens of our town are moral, religious, and refined, to an eminent degree; and, jealous of the reputation and welfare of their school, are giving their hearty support to its advancement. The buildings occupy an elevated position, and present a commanding appearance to our town and railroad. From the observatory on each, pupils have a fine view of the town and surrounding country.

Examination and Commencement Exercises

Then Annual Sermon will be preached on Sabbath, 13th, June. Examination, 14th and 15th.

Concert, 15th, at night.

Wednesday, 16th, the Graduation Essays, Commencement Address, and Conferring of Degrees.

236

Chapter 30 Excerpt

CATALOGUE OF THE IUKA FEMALE INSTITUTE AND IUKA MALE COLLEGE
1876–77

CATALOGUE

OF THE

IUKA FEMALE INSTITUTE

AND

IUKA MALE COLLEGE

IUKA, MISSISSIPPI, 1876 – 77

Memphis
S. C. Toof, Printer and Lithographer
1877

IUKA FEMALE INSTITUTE

BOARD OF TRUSTEES

George P. Hammerly, President.
A.T. Matthews, Esq.
Dr. J. A. Powell.
Col. R. W. Price.
Maj. Jas. M. Coman
Dr. J. S. Davis
Dr. Pugh Houston
Jas. H. Doan, Secretary

FACULTY

N. A. Flournoy, A. M., President.
Ancient Languages and Literature, English Language and Literature,
Mental and Moral Philosophy, and Book*keeping.

John C. Pettus, A. M., (U. Va.)
Modern Languages, Mathematics and Astronomy.

237

Miss M. Roselle Ferrill, M. A.,
Assistant in the Literary Departments, and Instructress of
Calisthenics.

Miss Hattie E. Lealand, M. M.,
Music Department

STUDENTS

Alexander, Innis	-	-	Tishomingo Co
Allen, Robert Ann	-	-	Iuka, Miss
Autrey, Annie	-	-	"
Bates, Marcella	-	-	"
Bates, Alice	-	-	"
Baumgarten, Emma	-	-	"
Barnett, Edga	-	-	"
Barnett, Shellie	-	-	"
Bevill, Georgie	-	-	"
Blythe, Ida	-	-	Tishomingo Co
Cayce, Annie	-	-	Iuka, Miss
Cayce, Minnie	-	-	"
Collins, Ada	-	-	"
Collins, Lizzie	-	-	"
Cunningham, Maggie	-	-	Booneville, Miss
Davis, Nannie	-	-	Iuka, Miss
Davis, Callie	-	-	"
Davis, Millie	-	-	"
Dean, Belle	-	-	"
Dean, Dixie	-	-	"
Dean, Della	-	-	"
Dean, Laura	-	-	"
Doan, Ottie	-	-	
Driver, Alice	-	-	Tishomingo Co
Driver, Ida	-	-	"
Ehert, George	-	-	Iuka, Miss
Ehert, Annie	-	-	"
Ellis, Lillie	-	-	"
Flake, Katie	-	-	
Goyer, Ida	-	-	Tishomingo Co
Ganong, Neely	-	-	Iuka, Miss
Gregson, Ora	-	-	"
Golden, Annie	-	-	"
Hammerly, Sallie	-	-	"
Hammerly, Mamie	-	-	"
Hammerly, Terry	-	-	"

Harris, Celeste	–	–	"
Hart, Mollie	–	–	"
Hart, Fannie	–	–	"
Harvey, Katie	–	–	"
Harvey, Thomas	–	–	"
Harvell, Mary	–	–	"
Heathman, Lawrence	–	–	"
Holleman, Mande	–	–	"
Hubbard, Annie	–	–	"
Hubbard, Ida	–	–	Tishomingo Co
Hutchins, Mary	–	–	Iuka, Miss
Hyatt, Anna Lee	–	–	"
Hyatt, Alice	–	–	"
Krause, Nora	–	–	"
Mackey, Ada	–	–	"
Mackey, Susie	–	–	"
Matthews, Dixie	–	–	"
Matthews, Anna Lou	–	–	"
Meaders, Flora	–	–	"
Merrill, Effie	–	–	"
Merrill, Helen	–	–	"
Merrill, Willie	–	–	"
Moore, J. H.	–	–	"
Moss, Belle	–	–	"
Nance, Minnie	–	–	"
Nance, Fannie	–	–	"
Paine, Ida	–	–	"
Pickrell, Emma	–	–	"
Powell, Mamie	–	–	"
Powell, Mattie	–	–	"
Powell, Emma	–	–	"
Rowles, Alice	–	–	"
Rowles, May	–	–	"
Rowles, Maggie	–	–	"
Simmons, Virginia	–	–	"
Sturdivant, Hattie	–	–	"
Thacker, Mollie	–	–	"
Whitfield, Lula	–	–	"
Woodley, Robert	–	–	Tishomingo Co
Worley, Laura	–	–	"
Worley, Annie	–	–	"
Worley, Alice	–	–	"
Total,	–	–	78

MUSIC CLASS

Bates, Marcella	Moss, Belle
Blythe, Ida	Nance, Minnie
Doan, Ottie	Powell, Mattie
Hammerly, Sallie	Rowles, Alice
Harris, Celeste	Rowles, Mamie
Matthews, Dixie	Simmons, Virginia
Merrill, Effie	Simmons, M. A. Jr.
Merrill, Helen	Worley, Annie

IUKA MALE COLLEGE

BOARD OF TRUSTEES

Col. R. W. Price, President.
Jno. Deavors.
Dr. Jno. A. Powell.
D. R. Hubbard.
Geo. P. Hammerly, Secretary.

FACULTY

John C. Pettus, A. M., (U. Va.) President
Ancient and Modern Languages, and Mathematics.

N. A. Flournoy, A. M.,
Book-keeping, Literature, Assistant in Ancient Languages &c

STUDENTS

Anderson, Robt.	–	–	Iuka, Miss
Barnett, Marshall	–	–	"
Barnett, William	–	–	"
Barnett, Thomas	–	–	"
Bates, Guy	–	–	"
Bates, Oliver	–	–	"
Baumgarten, Maxie	–	–	"
Bennett, Willie	–	–	Cherokee, Ala
Cayce, Marshall	–	–	Iuka, Miss
Crenshaw, Thomas	–	–	"
Crenshaw, Jeff	–	–	"
Doan, Wm. Banks	–	–	"
Doan, Samuel Lee	–	–	"

240

Dugger, W. F.	–	–	"
Ellis, S. Leonidas	–	–	"
Ganong, Thomas	–	–	"
Ganong, Eugene	–	–	"
Golden, Robert	–	–	"
Golden, Eugene	–	–	"
Gregson, John	–	–	"
Goyer, James	–	–	Tishomingo Co
Gellet, Oscar	–	–	Murfresboro, Tenn
Gellet, Otto	–	–	"
Gilbert, Alex	–	–	Tishomingo Co
Glover, Dorma	–	–	Iuka, Miss
Harris, R. L.	–	–	"
Harris, A. H.	–	–	"
Harris, E. W.	–	–	"
Hart, Robert	–	–	"
Holleman, James	–	–	"
Holmes, Harry	–	–	"
Houston, John	–	–	"
Hubbard, Thos. R.	–	–	"
Hubbard, John	–	–	"
Hunt, Nat.	–	–	Stanton, Tenn
McMahon, Thos.	–	–	Iuka, Miss
Miller, Hugh	–	–	"
Moss, James	–	–	"
Myrick, Newton	–	–	"
Paine, Walter	–	–	"
Pettus, F. H.	–	–	"
Pettus, J. C.	–	–	"
Pettus, W. J.	–	–	"
Pickrell, A. J.	–	–	"
Pickrell, John	–	–	"
Price, Thos.	–	–	"
Price, James	–	–	"
Reed, Emmet	–	–	"
Reed, Charles	–	–	"
Rice, James	–	–	"
Saffarrans, Thos.	–	–	"
Simmons, M.A., Jr	–	–	"
Smith, Alex.	–	–	Tishomingo Co
Thacker, Hartwell	–	–	Iuka, Miss
Warren, Clarke	–	–	"
Total,	–	–	56

COURSE OF INSTRUCTION

The Course of Instruction in both schools is the same, and embraces the Ancient, Modern, and English Languages, Mathematics, Book – keeping and the Sciences; and is divided into three departments, according to the advancement of the pupil, vis.: Primary, Academic and Collegiate. The design of each school is to give each pupil a thorough knowledge of the branches that he or she may study. At the close of each session, each pupil will be subjected to a rigid examination on each subject of study, and on completion of the Course of Study, provided the examination be satisfactory, will be awarded a Diploma of Graduation, and in case a pupil does not desire to take a full course, a Diploma on each study taken will be given, when a satisfactory examination has been undergone.

SESSIONS AND VACATIONS

The Scholastic Year is divided into two sessions of twenty weeks each. The Fall Session commences the First Monday in September, and continues twenty-one weeks. The Spring Session opens the Last Monday in January, and continues twenty weeks. No vacation will be given until the close of the Scholastic Year, with the exception of one week during Christmas, included in the Fall term of twenty-one weeks.

TERMS PER SESSION OF TWENTY WEEKS
(TO BE PAID MONTHLY.)

	PER MONTH
Primary Department, from	$2.00 to $3.00
Academic Department, from	$3.00 to $4.00
Collegiate Department,	$5.00
Music, (Instrumental,)	$6.00
Special Vocal Lessons with Piano,	$3.00
Calisthenics,	$1.00
Board, from	$12.00 to $15.00
Incidental Fee, per session,	$2.00
Diploma Fee, to be paid at Graduation	$5.00

LOCATION

Iuka, Mississippi, is one hundred and fifteen miles east of Memphis, on the Memphis and Charleston Railroad, in one of the most healthy portions of the South. The excellent mineral

242

waters of the place attract many visitors from various portions of the country. The community will compare favorably with any, being noted for its morality, refinement and hospitality.

CALENDAR OF 1877.

Examination of Classes, 7th, 8th, 11th and 12th of June.
Commencement Sermon, by Rev. G. W. Griffen, D. D.
Brownsville, Tenn., June 10th.
Exhibition Male College, June 11th, 8 P. M.
Calisthenic Exhibition, June 12th, 8 P. M.
Annual Address, by Dr. Griffin, June 13th, 10 A. M.
Concert and Graduation Exercises, June 13th, 8 P. M.

The Fall Sessions of 1877 will commence on First Monday in September.

Chapter 31 Excerpt

THE "IUKA MIRROR" SUPPLEMENT – M. A. SIMMONS, M.D.

Iuka is the county-seat of Tishomingo County, Mississippi, near the northeast corner of the State, on the Memphis and Charleston Railway, one hundred and fifteen miles east of Memphis, Tennessee, eight miles from steamboat navigation – at all stages of water – on the Tennessee River at Eastport, Mississippi. It is surrounded by high, hilly, healthy, good farming country. The water is all pure freestone, except an occasional chalybeate spring. There is a cluster of six medicinal springs near together in Iuka, that are much resorted to for their health and vigor restoring properties. On this subject we call the attention of medical men particularly to the following analysis of the waters of these springs, clipped from the "Iuka Mirror:"

Iuka Springs

For the gratification of our readers, we give the analysis of the water of these celebrated springs. Iuka is blessed with the finest chalybeate and sulphur waters, the private use of which is guaranteed to the schools and every citizen in the place. There are six of these springs, but only five have been analyzed, two by Eugene W. Hilgard, Geologist of the State of Mississippi, and three others by Drs. Gabbert and Morrow, of Memphis, Tennessee.

Box Spring No. 1 contains Peroxide of Iron in great abundance;
        Allumina small quantity;
        Chloride of Potassium;
        Chloride of Lime;
        Chloride of Sodium;
        Free Carbonic Acid;
        Sulphates of all proportions;

And is well adapted to all cases of debility, and is particularly applicable to dispepsia, liver disease and consumption, but contains rather too much iron for bowel derangements, unless the alum neutralizes the effect of the iron in such cases, which it will do if in sufficient quantity.

Box Spring No. 4 contains Protosulphate of Iron;
        Sulphate of Lime;

Sulphate of Soda;
Carbonate of Magnesia;
Chloride of Calcium;
Sulphate Allumina;
Earthly Phosphates;
Iodine combined with Magnesium slight trace.
A very valuable spring if properly used and perhaps better suited to cases of scrofula than either of the other.

Box Spring No. 5 contains Protoxide of Iron;
Chloride of Sodium;
Chloride of Calcium;
Sulphate of Lime;
Sulphate Magnesia;
Sulphate Soda;
Sulphurated Hydrogen Gas;
Carbonic Acid;
Anazotized matter mixed with Sulphur.
Also a valuable water and useful in all cases of female dibility from irregular action, dyspepsia, constipation and skin diseases. There are traces of other substances in these waters, but as the printers are hurrying us, we have no time to test for them.

L. W. GABBERT, M.D.
G. W. MORROW, M. D.

Gum Spring No. 2 contains Sulphurated Hydrogen largely;
Bicarbonate of Iron, largely;
Free Carbonic Acid; with small amounts of Bicarbonate of Magnesia;
Bicarbonate of Lime;
Bicarbonate of Potash and soda;
Chlorides of Potassium and Sodium;
It contains in 10,000 parts, 1.10 of solid ingredients, of which five-sixths at least are Peroxide of Iron.

Box Spring No. 3: Bicarbonate of Iron pretty largely;
Free Carbonic Acid, with very small amounts of Bicarbonate of Lime;
Bicarbonate of Magnesia;
Bicarbonate of Potash and Soda;
Sulphates of Potash and Soda;
Chlorides, a trace.

Gum Spring No. 2 is a strong "Red Sulphur" water.
Box Spring No. 3 is a simple Chalybeate, somewhat weaker,

245

it appears, than the former. Both differ from the majority of other Chalybeates and Sulphur waters of the State in their comparative freedom from purgative ingredients, which renders them better adapted to feeble patients, being almost purely tonic, and, in the case of the first mentioned, alternative.

EUGENE W. HILGARD
State Geologiest of Mississippi

Chapter 32 Excerpt

BROCHURE FOR THE IUKA NORMAL INSTITUTE IN 1883

IUKA NORMAL INSTITUTE

FOR BOTH SEXES.

—o—

Faculty.

H. A. DEAN, A.M., PRINCIPAL, and Prof. of
Latin, Greek, Metaphysics, School Government, Book-keeping, etc.

JOHN NEUHARDT, A. M., PRINCIPAL, and Prof. of
Mathematics, Nat. Sciences, Methods of Teaching, German, etc.

J. W. STILWELL, B.S., Prin. Preparatory Department

MRS. S. E. DEAN, M.A., Rhetoric

Miss MATTIE HARRIS, B.S., Intermediate Department.

Miss RUTH PENN, B.S., Primary Department.

.... Instrumental Music.

LAWRENCE STALLINGS, Librarian.

Calendar.

The Scholastic year is divided into four terms of ten weeks each.
Spring term begins Jan. 29, 1883. Summer term,
April 9, 1883. Fall term, Sept. 3, 1883.

Exposition and Commencement take place June 14 and 15, 1883.

Short term for Teachers begins June 18, 1883.

Location.

Iuka, Mississippi, noted for its healthful location, its
mineral springs, and for the generosity and hospitality of its
people, is situated on the Memphis and Charleston R. R.,
and hence is accessible from all points.

Terms and Expenses.

Tuition, $1.00 per week, in advance for ten weeks.
No Contingent Fee. No extra charges for any study except
Instrumental music which is $10 per term. Boarding and
Lodging, $10 per month. Pupils can enter any time, and
are charged from time of entrance. Diplomas granted, and
both bachelor and master degrees conferred.

****

NORMAL METHOD OF TEACHING RHETORIC.

The old method merits our attention first. By this method, the book (Rhetoric) is given the pupils, a lesson is assigned, they are told to read this-to study it-so as to be able to give the book answer to all questions, and lesson after lesson is gone over till the student's minds are crammed with a whole book full of definitions to be forgotten the next week after the annual examination. In connection with this book work, pupils are required to write not more than half a dozen essays. The teacher usually gives the subjects and advises the pupils to write their compositions without referring to books for information. Perhaps, the subject is one of which the student never heard, and thus the teacher requires his pupils to do what he himself could not do-that is, write an essay on an unfamiliar subject without going out of himself for information. In the higher institutions of learning, the method with a few lectures added is just about the same.

We can only give a skeleton of the Normal method and its results, yet all can see, after an examination, it to be the better way. Now, any one will admit that a man who knows, by name and at sight, the hoe, the plow, the reaper, the mule and the horse, and who does not at the same time know how to use and have them used would be a very poor farmer. Apply this practical idea to Rhetoric. One may recognize at sight and be able to name every principle of Rhetoric and not have the ability to use intelligently one of them even in a letter. The student should be able to recognize and use in a letter, newspaper article, or speech these principles. The power to use principles is the thing for which the student and teacher should work. The following is the natural or Normal method:

1. Let the teacher, logically, outline, for his class, several familiar subjects; then, give one - a tree, a table, a horse- to be outlined and brought in by the class, for

248

next day's lesson. Have some of the class to place this outline on the blackboard, and while this is being done, have read and discussed, by the class, some of the other outlines. Have the class to criticize and discuss those placed on the boards. Continue this work till each pupil has grasped the method of outlining and the logical idea running through all subjects. This is the key note.

2. Introduce composition work with letter writing- the simplest of all composition. Assign lesson in the book and let it be the chapter on epistolary correspondence. Recite book lesson and let pupils write, criticize and read the letters in class till every student can begin and close a letter decently.

3. Pass to simple narration. Request each pupil to select an excursion or a visit, no matter what, so it is an actual occurrence. Direct pupils to write incidents in a chronological order. While these are being written and read in class, study and recite the chapters of the book on narration.

4. Make for the class a general outline for writing biographical sketches, and show the class how to use this in making an outline for a sketch of a particular individual. Give subjects for biographical sketches, and add variety by giving as subjects natural objects to be described. Continue book work on biography and description and in writing on different subjects. Have all essays read and criticized in class. Use the technicalities of the science and encourage the class to do the same.

5. Give debatable subjects, assign pupils to affirmative and negative. Have the class to study and recite the chapters of the book on debate. Have their arguments pro and con read, criticized and decided by the class.

6. Methods of criticism. The teacher must arrange a scale for criticism-errors to be indicated by numbers--then have all compositions read in class and criticized by the class. Let pupils exchange essays, examine and report criticisms in class. After this the teacher should criticize the compositions and return them to the class for examination or to be copied. The teacher should never correct a composition till it has been read to the class.

7. By this method the class in five months will recite, read and criticize about one composition per week, do all the book work necessary, make an outline-the preacher's notes or the lawyer's brief-on about forty subjects, and thus each pupil investigates closely about sixty subjects while learning the Rhetorical definitions.

8. Results of the method to the student. 1. He learns to spell practically. 2. His vocabulary is greatly increased. 3. His penmanship is improved. 4. He is constantly gaining information, increasing his powers of understanding and appreciating our best writers. 5. He cultivates a taste for reading, and dime novels cease to be in demand. 6. His elocutionary powers are developed, for each essay is a reading lesson is native pride is aroused and his successes and failures are pointed out to him by his classmates. 7. He acquires a practical knowledge of English Grammar. 8. He gains a logical method of study. 9. He has a practical knowledge of Rhetoric, which combined with his ability to investigate a subject, to write it up and to read or deliver it to an audience, makes him a common sense Rhetorician -the point to be gained.

GENERAL LITERATURE.

The normal method of teaching "General Literature" is unique. It is practical. After one acquires enough Arithmetic to make ordinary business calculations, General Literature is perhaps the most practical study found in any curriculum. We want to talk, with strangers and friends on subjects connected with English History, English Social Life, Novels, Poetry, Theology, Politics and the Biographies of our great men ten thousand times to one, where our higher mathematics, Ancient and Modern languages would be a suitable subject for conversation. A student studying English authors properly guided, can become familiar with Ancient, Medieval and Modern history before he can become acquainted with the history of Greece and Rome through their languages. We would not reject these languages from a finished education, but we would pay more attention to Literature as a study to develop the powers of our pupils and make them practical men and women.

We will contrast the old and the new methods, and compare their results, so that all can see the, better way and know where to find it. Colleges and universities have from one to three literary societies-usually secret; Normal schools have

250

debating sections-never secret. All the registered pupils in the first are never members of these literary, secret societies; all pupils in Normal schools, without pressure from the faculty, become active members of the debating sections. In the college societies, the number of members is so great that a pupil has but few opportunities during the year for exercising his powers in debate; debating sections are always small, (10 to 15 members,) and the student thus gets to study and discuss a subject each week. Hence he pretty thoroughly investigates about forty subjects each year. College societies too often meet for fun and frolic; the debating sections meet for actual literary work. College societies are frequently hot-beds of rowdyism and insubordination; normal debating sections, a teacher usually being present, have a powerful influence over pupils for good. The subjects are, by the pupils, selected at random; in the other, the subjects are selected by the teacher. In the first the student is at a loss as to what book to refer for information; in the second, the teacher gives the subject and the references necessary to enable the pupil to acquit himself creditably. In college societies, the members of the faculty put themselves to no trouble to teach parliamentary law; in the normal sections, a teacher, from time to time, gives special drills in parliamentary usages.

Results obtained. In colleges, the secret societies are suppressed in many instances; in normal debating sections, the teacher and members are frequently on an equal footing, the teacher being placed on debate. Only brassy, gasy members gain much power in debate, in these secret societies; the members of normal debating sections develop all their powers. They learn to stand on their feet and to think logically and speak cogently. From the first, the student at graduation has an excellent knowledge of Latin and Greek, the dead past; from the second, at the same time, the pupil has an excellent knowledge of Latin and Greek and is actually familiar with the current thought and history of his own country.

This literary work is further carried on in Normal schools by giving to students historical, scientific, political and theological subjects on which to prepare and deliver speeches, each ten weeks, before the whole school and others, thus cultivating the power to entertain an audience and to give pupils confidence in themselves. Again, this literary work is continued after the subject of Rhetoric is finished. Students are organized into what we call advanced Rhetoric sections. Subjects on which they write essays are given to each member of these sections. These essays are read, criticized in class, exchanged and closely criticized by pupils and finally, by the teachers. Students thus write, read and criticize, three to five essays, each ten weeks.

Now, anyone can see that, if the Normal method of teaching Rhetoric and "General Literature," is carried out, a class of twenty pupils would in three years become somewhat familiar with nearly all the important subjects in the whole range of human knowledge. But some may claim that this method leaves no time for other studies. The power and enthusiasm gained in this department of education has an immense reflex action and enables students to master the other studies more rapidly than on the old method.

NATURAL SCIENCES

Are taught practically by means of apparatus, experimenting, illustrating, collecting specimens, analyzing, classifying outlining. Our "Development'" methods, the result of professional study and philosophical investigation, are scientific and practical. The student should understand the principles upon which a science is founded, and its relations to other sciences, as well as that of each of its parts. This is acquired in our work by means of Topical and Outline methods. But he must also aim at practical power, not only be master of the theory but the practice, not only able to think, but to do. This power is secured from judicious use of apparatus and discussion by the pupil, under the direction of the teacher in the laboratory. The best way to teach a pupil to think is to exercise him in the actual expression of thought, and the best way to teach him any principle in science is to put him to investigating, experimenting, observing and concluding.

To illustrate our methods more specifically, suppose a class in Philosophy is studying Pneumatics--Compressibility and Elasticity of the air. Before dismissing the class, the teacher requests each member to make a Pop-gun for to-morrow's lesson. Every pupil will at once express a great desire for this kind of play. The teacher, or a pupil, assisted by the members of the class, will then put the following outline on the blackboard:

252

POP-GUN.

    1^1 Parts.
    2^1 Experiment.
    3^1 Observation.
    4^1 Conclusion.

This outline being copied by the members, the teacher requests them to experiment, observe the results, draw their own conclusions, so as to be ready to complete the outline and deliver a lecture on Compressibility and Elasticity of air, when called upon, at the next recitation.

At the next recitation, some are sent to the board to write down their outlines, others criticize and compare notes. The outline, enlarged or completed, will then stand as follows :

POP-GUN.

    1^1 Parts.

        1^2 Tube or Cylinder.
        2^2 Ramrod.
        3^2 Paper or Lint Wads.

    2^1 Experiment.

        1^2 Put a wad in one end of tube.
        2^2 Put a wad in the other end.
        3^2 Force one through the tube with ramrod.

    3^1 Observation.

        1^2 The other wad is projected.
        2^2 One wad remains in tube.
        3^2 A loud report is heard.

    4^1 Conclusion.

        1^2 The air in the tube was compressed.
        2^2 The compressed air expanded and
            threw out the wad.
        3^2 Hence, air is compressible and elastic.

One of the pupils is now called upon to lecture from this outline, and experiment with his pop gun, while the others

253

criticize all the errors that are made and suggest facts that are omitted in the discussion.

From the above, any person of ordinary intelligence may see the superiority of our methods to those generally pursued in colleges. Other subjects are taught on similar plans. The upward pressure of the air may be illustrated by "sucking water" through a straw or with a tumbler of water and a piece of paper. The downward pressure may be proved by the action of a common leather-sucker. Hundred other principles in science may be illustrated and proved with such experiments and apparatus as the student can easily per form and make. Not the Professors, but our Students, do the lecturing and experimenting, and thus they acquire power and thoroughness in the Physical Sciences. We thus secure such enthusiasm, that there is comparatively no time for disorder and idleness. Study is made a source of enjoyment, and each pupil is excited to a determined effort to make the most of his time. We give subjects to be investigated, not books to be memorized. By this determined, self-reliant co-operation, our pupils are able to acquire a thorough and practical education here in half the time usually required under the old system.

TRAINING DEPARTMENT.

This department is as essential to the profession of teaching as a medical school is to the profession of medicine. We make a specialty of this work and challenge competition.

The subjects and branches adapted to the teacher's wants are thoroughly mastered. These are outlined by the pupils, and thoroughly discussed and illustrated. The principles of education or of the natural development of the mind are mastered and exemplified in all their bearings and relations. Some of these are,

1. Activity is a law of childhood; accustom the child to do.

2. Cultivate the faculties in their natural order; first form the mind and then furnish it.

3. Begin with the senses and the known, and never tell a child what he can discover for himself.

4. Let every lesson have a point.

5. Develop the idea, then give the term.

6. Synthesis, then analysis.

7. Teach the subject, and not the book.

8. Reach the mind through as many senses as possible.

9. Develop the memory through the understanding.

10. Never demand work without a preliminary drill to remove doubts and difficulties.

With these principles thoroughly assimilated in his mind, the pupil-teacher is put to actual work in teaching the various branches. He takes the place of teacher, for the time being, and manages a class under the eyes of the principal and fellow teachers. His errors are then pointed out, and his excellencies commended. This course of Practical Training in the several branches forms, more than any thing else, the prominent and distinctive feature of the Normal school. Based on reason and the principles of the mind, the young teacher becomes a skillful master in the art of teaching. He accumulates the experiences of years in the school room, bursts the shackles of routine work and fogyism, becomes original and a living, acting self, and knows how to develop and contrive methods suited to the particular schools he may teach. With him, no experiments and failures need be made on precious, immortal souls; for he is master of his situation.

Every attention is given to the means and methods of organizing, governing and managing country district-schools, as well as graded or union schools. Nothing, essential to the skill and success of the teacher, from the forms of making contracts with directors to the highest duty and responsibility, is omitted in the Training Department. The demand for practical power is nowhere felt more sensibly than in our common schools. There is a deplorable lack of special training among teachers. Our schools should surely be filled with something better than those who have failed in every other calling. There must be professional training. The demand comes from all parts of the country, not for more but for better teachers-teachers who know how to teach. The dignity and responsibility of the work demand it; the parents who must entrust their treasures to the teacher demand it; and the little hearts and minds, impoverished and dwarfed by

255

false methods or rather no methods, demand it in tones the public ear dares not ignore.

By spending one, or more terms under Normal instruction and training, teachers may expect to receive an immediate increase of wages from twenty to fifty per cent, besides enjoying the consciousness of increased usefulness.

Chapter 33 Excerpts

IUKA NORMAL INSTITUTE BOOKLET 1883-84
LIST OF STUDENTS AND GRADUATES

Undergraduates (set to begin a new term on September 3, 1883)

Adams, Hooper	–	Sumner Co., Tenn.
Anderson, Jimmie	–	Tishomingo Co., Miss
Aydlett, James	–	"
Aydlett, Mamie	–	"
Aydlett, Wissie	–	"
Brown, B. W.	–	Dyer Co., Tenn.
Boyd, Collins	–	Tishomingo Co., Miss.
Blythe, K.	–	"
Blythe, Ida	–	"
Blythe, Jeff	–	"
Buck, Mrs.	–	Noxubee Co., Miss.
Clopton, Irene	–	Tishomingo Co., Miss.
Clopton, James	–	"
Choate, Willie	–	"
Choate, Lucy	–	"
Choate, James	–	"
Choate, Willie	–	"
Choate, Robert	–	"
Castleberry, James	–	"
Castleberry, Babe	–	"
Covington, May Lou	–	Tippah Co., Miss.
Durham, Laetta	–	"
Dean, Dixie	–	Tishomingo Co., Miss.
Dean, Della	–	"
Dean, Laura	–	"
Dean, Sidney	–	"
Dean, Whitney	–	"
Dean, Lawrence	–	"
Dean, Annie	–	Dyer Co., Tenn.
Drake, Eddie	–	Tishomingo Co., Miss.
Drake, Ida	–	"
Drake, Robert	–	"
Davis, Mollie	–	"
Davis, Ella	–	"
Davis, Hattie	–	"
DeWoody, Linnie	–	"

257

DeWoody, Bettie	–	"
Doan, S. L.	–	Memphis, Tenn.
Doan, Livia	–	Panola Co., Miss.
Deavours, Stony	–	Tishomingo Co., Miss.
Deavours, John	–	"
Eddings, Carrie	–	Coahoma Co., Miss.
Ellis, Eddie	–	Tishomingo Co., Miss.
Fairley, Florence	–	Jefferson Co., Miss.
Farmer, H. M.	–	Lowndes Co., Miss.
Gist, Mattie	–	Tishomingo Co., Miss.
Gist, Mollie	–	"
Gist, Fannie	–	"
Gregson, Ora	–	"
Gregson, Wm.	–	"
Glover, Dormand	–	"
Glover, Minnie	–	"
Glover, George	–	"
Giles, Morton	–	"
Gewin, Jessie	–	"
Gewin, William	–	"
Gewin, H. L.	–	"
Ganong, Willie	–	"
Ganong, Louis	–	"
Ganong, Stone	–	"
Ganong, Nealy	–	"
Ganong, Robert	–	"
Ganong, John	–	"
Ganong, Julia	–	"
Hart, Robert	–	Texas
Hart, Eddie	–	Nashville, Tenn.
Hubbard, Sallie	–	Tishomingo Co., Miss.
Hubbard, Laura	–	"
Hubbard, J. B.	–	"
Hubbard, Annie	–	"
Hubbard, Lena	–	"
Hubbard, Maggie	–	"
Hubbard, Minnie	–	"
Hubbard, Clarance	–	"
Hubbard, Hattie	–	"
Hubbard, Willie	–	"
Hubbard, Josie	–	"
Harvey, Katie	–	"
Harvey, Tom	–	"
Houston, John	–	"
Houston, Ella	–	"
Harvey, Corrie	–	"

258

Hammerly, Terry	–	"
Hammerly, M. B.	–	Tishomingo Co., Miss
Hammerly, Delia	–	"
Hammerly, Laura	–	"
Hughes, Annie	–	"
Harris, Celeste	–	"
Harris, Lillie	–	"
Hodges, Harry	–	Lee County, Ark.
Holmes, Robert	–	Tishomingo Co., Miss.
Holmes, Julia	–	"
Hill, James	–	"
Hill, Myrtie	–	"
Hill, Annie	–	"
Houston, Moses	–	"
Houston, Julia	–	"
Harrison, Leon	–	"
Harrison, Willis	–	"
Hyatt, Tom	–	"
Hyatt, Alice	–	"
Hyatt, Mamie	–	"
Hyatt, Annie	–	"
Hamilton, J. P.	–	Lincoln Co., Tenn.
Jourdan, James	–	Tishomingo Co., Miss.
Jourdan, Minnie	–	"
Johnson, Irene	–	"
Jones, Willie	–	"
Kraus, Nora	–	"
Kraus, Alice	–	"
Keth, Bert	–	"
Kimberley, Sam	–	"
Luker, Clara	–	"
Lovelace, Eland	–	"
Lovelace, Marietta	–	"
Long, Fred	–	"
Long, Horrace	–	"
Long, Adolphus	–	"
Leatherwood, Sallie	–	"
Lockwood, Maggie	–	"
Linton, J. H.	–	"
Linton, E. S.	–	"
Moss, Belle	–	"
Moss, Mollie	–	"
Moss, Doan	–	"
Moss, Robert	–	"
Moss, Coleman	–	"
Matthews, Annie	–	"

Matthews, Pritcherd	–	"
McKinney, Ella	–	Tishomingo Co., Miss
McKinney, Ed	–	"
McKinney, Willis	–	"
McKinney, Carrie	–	"
McKinney, Sallie	–	"
Murrell, May	–	"
Murrell, Bettie	–	"
Murrell, Julia	–	"
Merrill, Willie	–	"
Merrill, Lila	–	"
Moore, William	–	Crockett Co., Tenn.
Moore, Russell	–	Tishomingo Co., Miss.
Moore, Hafford	–	"
Moore, Hardy	–	"
Mackey, Susie	–	"
McMahon, T. J.	–	"
Miles, Belle	–	"
Miles, Annie	–	"
Miller, Ermine	–	Claiborne Co., Miss.
Milseps, Alice	–	Tishomingo Co., Miss.
Miller, Lillie	–	"
Neblet, Fletcher	–	"
Neblet, Ada	–	"
O'Malley, Mary	–	"
O'Malley, Mattie	–	"
O'Malley, Maggie	–	"
O'Malley, Edgar	–	"
Odom, Jed	–	"
Penn, Florence	–	Gibson Co., Tenn.
Powell, May	–	Tishomingo Co., Miss.
Powell, Emma	–	"
Powell, Albert	–	"
Powell, Julia	–	"
Prince, Sidney	–	Clay County, Miss.
Pledge, Katie	–	Hardeman Co., Tenn
Pledge, Birdie	–	"
Puryear, Addie	–	Lawrence Co., Ala.
Reynolds, B	–	Tishomingo Co., Miss.
Reynolds, Fannie	–	"
Reynolds, S	–	"
Reynolds, W	–	"
Rice, Ida	–	"
Rice, Lonie	–	"
Rice, Ed	–	"
Rice, Rossie	–	"

260

Rice, G.	–	"
Reeves, Annie	–	Crockett Co., Tenn.
Richeson, Alpha	–	Gibson Co., Tenn.
Reed, Charley	–	Tishomingo Co., Miss.
Sills, Ella	–	Shelby Co., Tenn.
Seay, May	–	Tishomingo Co., Miss.
Seay, Annie	–	"
Seay, Ketie	–	"
Stallings, Lawrence	–	Gibson County, Tenn.
Stallings, Bryant	–	"
Stell, Frank	–	Tishomingo Co., Miss.
Smith, Oscar	–	"
Smith, Cora	–	"
Stone, Annie	–	"
Stoune, Willie	–	Colbert County, Ala.
Sawyers, Lizzie	–	Tishomingo Co., Miss.
Sawyers, James	–	"
Sawyers, Addie	–	"
Sawyers, Newland	–	"
Summers, Mattie	–	"
Stone, Linnie	–	Chester Co., Tenn.
Simmons, Eleazer	–	Tishomingo Co., Miss.
Tullock, N	–	"
Tullock, Lee	–	"
Trenthan, Mamie	–	"
Tuggle, J. P.	–	Gibson Co., Tenn.
Throckmorton, Willie	–	Memphis, Tenn.
Throckmorton, James	–	"
Trimble, Linda	–	Tishomingo Co., Miss.
Walker, Birdie	–	"
Walker, Lula	–	"
Walker, Susie	–	Colbert Co., Ala.
Whitefield, Lula	–	Tishomingo Co., Miss.
Wood, Mary	–	"
Wood, Edna	–	"
Wood, Floyd	–	"
Wood, Rose	–	"
Wood, Lenora	–	"
Wood, Luther	–	"
Wood, Ella	–	"
Wood, Emmet	–	"
Weaver, Idona	–	"
Weaver, John	–	"
Weaver, Annie	–	"
Williams, Baleus	–	"
Williams, Belle	–	"

261

Williams, Frank	–	"
Williams, Marcus	–	Tishomingo Co., Miss
Wingo, Shellie	–	"
Wingo, Ed	–	"
Wingo, Annie	–	"
Word, P. B.	–	"
Woodal, John	–	"
Woodal, Mary	–	"
Woodal, Mamie	–	"
Woodal, Jennie	–	"
Wormsley, Lizzie	–	"
Wormsley, Myrtie	–	"
Wormsley, John	–	"
White, J. C.	–	LaFayette Co. Miss.

Chapter 39 Excerpts

IUKA NORMAL INSTITUTE 1898
COMMENCEMENT EXERCISES

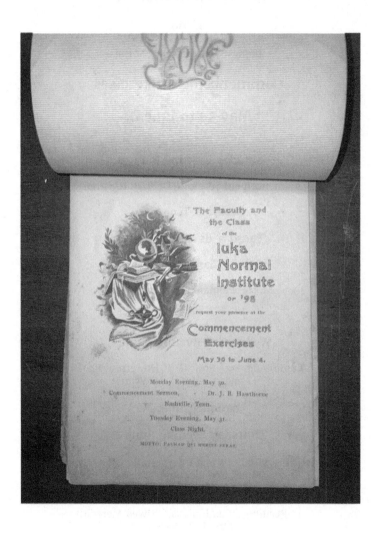

The Faculty and
the Class

of the

Iuka Normal Institute

of '98

request your presence at the

Commencement Exercises

May 30 to June 4.

Monday Evening May 30.

Commencement Sermon –Dr. J. B. Hawthorne

Nashville, Tennessee,

Tuesday Evening, May 31.

Class Night.

Motto: Palmam Qui Meruit Ferat

*****

Wednesday Evening, June 1.

Alumni Address –Prof. G. T. Howerton, Ph. D.
Essayist. –Mrs. J. M Wyatt

Banquet, 10 P. M.

Thursday Evening, June 2.

Artistic Presentations and Interpretations by Advanced
Music and Elocution Classes

1. Reading, "Aux Italieus,"–Owen Meredith
Mrs. R. L. Shook.

2. Onomatopoetic, Tennyson's "Bugle Song," Class

7. Humorous Drama, "Place aux Dames."

DRAMATIC PERSONAE.

"Ophelia," Mattie Watson.
"Portia," Birdie Dugger
"Juliet," Zola McIntire
"Lady Macbeth," Mrs. McIntire

8. Greek Romance, from the German by Frederick Helm.
"Parthenai," Miss Victoria McCay.
"Ingomar," J. E. Blythe.

9. Reading, "Minister's Housekeeper," - H. B. Stowe

10. Shaftsbury Tableaux Plastique, - Class

Louise E. Anthony, Directress of Music
L. Pierce H. McIntire, Directress of Expression

Friday Evening, June 3.

Annual Address,-Hon. Chas. E. Hooker
Jackson, Mississippi

CLASS ROLL

Jourdan E. Blythe, A. B., President
Jas. C. Russell, B. S., Vice-President
C.L. Dobbs, B. S., Secretary and Treas.

Jas. C. Russell, B.S.,   )
Jas. L. McKeown, A. B.,   ) Reception Committee
William M. Riddle, B.S.,   )

Knowles S. Archer, B. S.
Robt L. Shook, B.S.
Robt P. Cameron, A. B.
Chas. R. Freeman. A. B.

265

Chapter 42 Excerpt

IUKA NORMAL INSTITUTE
1901 INVITATION TO GRADUATION

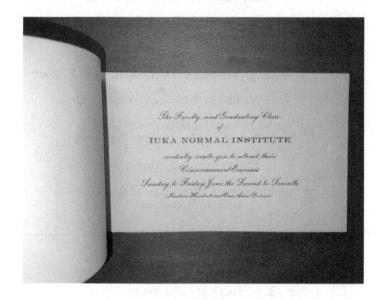

The Faculty and Graduation Class

of

IUKA NORMAL INSTITUTE

cordially invite you to attend their

Commencement Exercises

Sunday to Friday, June the Second to Seventh

Nineteen Hundred and One Anne Domini

**

General Programme

Baccalaureate Sermon

Rev. W. A. Hamlett - - - Grenada, Miss.

Methodist Episcopal Church

Sunday, June Second, Eleven A.M.

—

Class Reception Monday
June Third, Eight P.M.

—

Alumni Address
Hon. J. A. E. Pyle – Iuka, Miss.

Alumni Essay
Mrs. T. M. McDonald – Iuka, Miss.

Tuesday, June Fourth,
Eight-Thirty P.M.

—

Alumni Banquet
Wednesday, June Fifth, Nine P.M.

—

Graduating Orations
Thursday, June Sixth, Eight-Thirty P.M.

—

Baccalaureate Address
Hon. E. S. Candler – Corinth, Miss.
and
Degrees Conferred
June Seventh, Eight-Thirty P.M.

Class Roll

Mr. Townes R. Leigh, President
Miss Delia Downing, Secretary
Mr. Guy D. Haskins, Treasurer

Reception Committee

Mr. John O. Gurney
Mr. Carl Ferrell
Mr. Christ H. Roman
Mr. Estelle Dobbs
Miss Maud Reid

Motto
Cordam Et Mentem Colamus

Colors
Canary and Blue

Flower
Jessamine

****

THE END

****

Index

Index

271

273

275

McDonald home v, vi, x, 1, 32, 33, 36, 157, 221

McDonald, Mrs. T. M. (Miss Lyla) v, vi, 1, 14, 142, 157, 170, 208, 210, 212, 221, 260, 267, 295, 296

McDonald, Theodore Lyle "Ted" 296

McDonald, Thomas Marion (Lyla's Husband) vi, vii, 32, 157, 221, 295, 296

McDonald, Thomas Merrill 157, 296

McIntire, H. 137, 265

McIntire, Mrs. 137, 265

McIntire, Zola 137, 265

McIntosh, Billie 224

McIntosh, Laura J. 224

McIntosh, Mattie 225

McIntosh, (Rev.) William 62, 73

McIntosh, Willie 225

McKeown, Jas. L. 265

McKeown, Rev. L. A. 65

McKinley, President 135

McKinney and Weaver 85

McKinney, Ann 225

McKinney, Carrie 260

McKinney, Ed 260

McKinney, Ella 260

McKinney, J. B. 17, 67, 84, 225

McKinney, Sallie 260

McKinney, W. E. 22

McKinney, Willis 260

McKnight and Son 17

McKnight, C. W. 68

McKnight Home 31, 39, 67, 68, 81, 152

McKnight, Linda J. 225

McKnight, Mrs. C. W. 152

McKnight, Mrs. John 67

McKnight, R. L 20, 21

McKnight, William 17, 31, 67, 68

McMahon, Laura 229

McMahon, Thos. 241

McMahon, T. J. 260

McMechan & Coman 24

McNairy County, Tennessee 192, 225

McNairy, Tennessee 224

McPeters 72

McPeters, Mattie 225

McRae, Ben 208

McRae, B. F. 67, 68

McRae, Dr. 200

McRae, Dr. E. F. 161

McRae, Jr., Ben F. 208

McRee, Jr., R. A. 208

McTeire, (Bishop) 60, 61

Meaders, Flora 239

Meaders, Rev. G. R. 65

Meek, (Colonel) S. M. 131

Meeks, Mattie 225

Memphis and Charleston Railroad 18, 33, 45, 50, 51, 52, 59, 67, 70, 71, 72, 78, 88, 138, 174, 187, 217, 218, 235, 242, 244, 247

Memphis and La Grange Railroad 58, 218

Memphis and Little Rock Railroad 52

Memphis Appeal 48

Memphis Conference Preachers 64

Memphis, Tennessee 16, 19, 29, 33, 34, 52, 53, 57, 58, 71, 95, 166, 178, 185, 194, 199, 213, 214, 215, 219, 228, 235, 237, 242, 244, 258, 261

Merrill, Birdie 157

285

R

Railway Employees Journal 179, 195

Ramsey, (Reverend) E. B. 69

Ramsey, T. Y. 65

Randolph, (Rev.) J. B. 65

Ray, Dabney 84

Red Bay, Alabama 159

Red Sulphur Springs 194

Reed, Anna Lou Matthews 66, 199, 229, 239

Reed, Charles 241

Reed, Charley 261

Reed, Emmet 241

Reed, E. N. 45

Reed, Mrs. E. N. 149, 199

Reeves, Annie 261

Reeves, Mollie 226

Reid, Annette 175

Reid, Miss Maud 267

Reno, Birdie 68, 226

Reno, Lula 68

Reno, Minnie 68

Reno, Mr. Emmet 68

Reporter, (The) - Newspaper 12

Revolutionary War 192

Reynolds, B. 260

Reynolds, Fannie 260

Reynolds, S. 260

Reynolds, W. 260

Rice, Addie 230

Rice, Ed 260

Rice, Ervie 230

Rice, G. 261

Rice, Ida 230, 260

Rice, James 241

Rice, Lonie 260

Rice, Rossie 260

Rice, Zenia 230

Richardson, Isabella 225

Richards, Sarah 82

Richeson, Alpha 261

Rick's Home 93

Riddle, William M. 265

Rienzi, Mississippi 13, 78

Ringold, Laura 230

Ringold, Mary 230

Riverton, Alabama 28, 29, 79, 190

Riverton Junction 190

Robertson, (General) 5, 6

Robinson, J. I. 118

Robinson, John 30, 209

Robinson, Luke 208

Robinson, Mollie 226

Robinson, Rev. J. R. 65

Rockford, Illinois 22

Roddey, (General) 22, 83, 84, 85, 86

Roddey's Cavalry 22

Roddey's Command 22, 40, 84, 85, 86, 87

Roman, Mr. Christ H. 267

Rome, Georgia 86

Rose Cottage 40

Rosecrans, (General) 35, 45, 46, 47, 53, 90, 91, 93

Rose Trail (The) 19

Ross, Helen 225

Ross, Jennie 226

Ross' Landing 6

Rowles, Alice 230, 239, 240

Rowles, Maggie 230, 239

Rowles, Mamie 240

Rowles, Mary 230

Rowles, May 239

Rudd's Ferry 192

Rushing, Mrs. K. L. 207

Russell, Jas. C. 265

Rutledge, Mrs. R. T. 152

About the Authors

Billie Burke (that's how everyone knew her)

Years ago, in reference to many things in general and about nothing in particular, our mother (Billie Burke Whitehurst Thomas) cast a knowing grin atop that awe-inspiring smile of hers as she said to me, "One day you'll understand." I wasn't sure what she meant or even if she really knew something I didn't yet know, but the statement and that knowing grin stuck with me.

Billie Burke Whitehurst Thomas in her den pondering Christmas cards and the like in the chair and under the light where she studied and organized Miss Lyla's box of old papers in the 1990s.

The glint in her eye suggested people have worth, people have value, all people. That is a difficult concept for an adult, much less for a child, to wrap his mind around. Nonetheless, I've come to feel it is a significant step in helping people realize their potential and find a unique purpose in life.

Along the way, Mom also told me, "You can't change the world." At the time and for a good time hence, I wished she hadn't said that. It stifled my even making the effort. Perhaps it's linked to "One day you'll understand." You can't change the world, doesn't mean the world can't be changed or redirected, but it points to change being both a personal and a collective effort. Our parents' generation, during WWII, actively and collectively defended democracy against authoritarianism. Their struggle was real. Their hopeful gift to the world shown for generations.

This hallmark of that generation was real and filling. So when Mom pondered Miss Lyla's Papers, it was sincere and went on for years. She even made this effort look enjoyable, but when pressed about how it was going, she would say, "Miss Lyla just says the same thing over and over again." Of course that was true. Miss Lyla held this story close to her heart and seemed to search for the perfect way to tell it throughout her life.

Mom's health declined over the years, into her 80s, 90s and beyond 100. She knew there was something she was supposed to finish but couldn't quite remember what it was.

Eddie Thomas (next in line on this mission)
I won't go into too much detail about Eddie. You know him rather well already through his presentations in this book. I will say that he is one of those people who can sit down and write a long, detailed and interesting letter or email faster than I can come up with a subject/title. He's quick. So the fact that he has spent as much time as

Mom did (or more) working on this book points to how big the task has been to turn this box of old papers into a book. Suffice it to say that this book would never have come about had it not been for Eddie (and Billie Burke and Miss Lyla, of course).

Frank Thomas (me)

It's not that I don't get and appreciate the lesson Mom exhibited by making an effort to share Miss Lyla's passion (papers) posthumously. My energy level for those tasks can wane due to distractions and the time required. However, I am a puzzle person and can enthusiastically get involved with the challenge of a good puzzle like Miss Lyla's papers. Near the end of the task, this book needed some technical assistance to help get it organized into a printable layout with a decent index and the like that might help it get to press. You need a guy to fit a square peg into a round hole? I'm your man.

Lyla McDonald

Miss Lyla lies at the heart of this book; I'm tempted to say, "Bless her heart." Aside from being that "cheerleader," as Eddie calls her, for our small town, she is also one of those landmark characters in the timeline of our community. BUT... she was also a wife and a mother. She married Tom McDonald on Valentine's Day in 1899. An article about their wedding entitled *A Nice Valentine* contains the following quote taken from the Vidette: "Of Miss Lyla it can be truthfully said that Iuka has no sweeter or womanly young lady or one more generally beloved and respected for her many charming qualities."

Tom and Lyla had four children:

Two Daughters
Mildred M. McDonald (Dycus)
Elizabeth McDonald (Gerbig)

Two Sons
Thomas Merrill McDonald
Theodore Lyle McDonald

A picture of Elizabeth as a young girl found among Miss Lyla's Papers is in this book on page 174. Mildred, Elizabeth and Thomas as children can be seen on page 157. Theodore, "Ted," despite reaching adulthood, possessed the mind of a child, and though this undoubtedly presented challenges for Lyla and Tom, they were there for "Ted" throughout their lives.

* * *

The release date for Miss Lyla's Papers is Valentine's Day 2024, 125 years to the day after Lyla and Tom McDonald married, and it comes 100 years after the publication of Miss Lyla's first book about Iuka. Miss Lyla's Papers, published 62 years after her death in 1962, isn't likely to win great awards or notable attention. Still, if you have followed along to this point, you know these tales form the bedrock of a small community in the hills of Tishomingo County, Mississippi.

I am confident Miss Lyla would want you to realize, whoever you are and wherever you are from, that you are part of a community. If you can't yet feel that community in your heart, be patient with yourself and explore once again this magical spot Miss Lyla held dear. Know that she is encouraging you to find those experiences that bind us and make our world a better place.

Made in the USA
Las Vegas, NV
02 August 2024

93296506R00174